C000125288

BIZARRE

TRUE CRIME

VOLUME 4

Ben Oakley

Twelvetrees Camden

Copyright © 2021 Ben Oakley

Bizarre True Crime Volume 4

ISBN: 9798485904647

Independently published.

All rights reserved.

No part of this book may be reproduced, or stored in a retrieval system, or transmitted in any form or by any means, electronic, mechanical, photocopying, recording, or otherwise, without express written permission of the publisher.

Each case has been fully researched and fact-checked to bring you the best stories possible and all information is correct at the time of publication. This book is meant for entertainment and informational purposes only.

The author or publisher cannot be held responsible for any errors or misinterpretation of the facts detailed within. The book is not intended to hurt or defame individuals or companies involved.

Cover design by Ulrich B.

Discover more:

www.benoakley.co.uk

"I would rather entertain and hope that people learned something than educate people and hope they were entertained." - Walt Disney

Also by Ben Oakley

True Crime

Bizarre True Crime Series

The Monstrous Book of Serial Killers

Giant True Crime Books

True Crime 365

Year of the Serial Killer

Harrison Lake Mysteries

Beyond the Blood Streams

Perfect Twelve

Monster of the Algarve

Subnet Series

Unknown Origin

Alien Network

Final Contact

Other Fiction

The Mystery of Grimlow Forest

Mental Health

Suicide Prevention Handbook

Bizarre True Crime Volume 4

20 bonkers and ghastly true crime stories.

1. The Villisca Axe Murders

In a town known as the pretty place, an entire family were killed by an axeman who had been hiding in their attic waiting for them to go to sleep, in a case that continues to haunt to this day.

2. Truth Stranger than Fiction

A detective reads a self-published fiction novel and discovers similarities to a real murder three years earlier, along with clues in the book that only the real killer would have known.

3. The Uncatchable

A man known as the Greek Robin Hood, went on a 30-year crime spree, gave money to the poor, twice broke out of prison with a helicopter, and broke into prison to rescue his brother – with a tank.

4. Truman Library Robbery

Thieves broke into the Presidential Library and stole a selection of ceremonial swords and daggers worth over $1million – in under 45 seconds – leading to theories the items were stolen to order.

5. Black Mass of the Fortune Teller

Black magic, witchcraft, poisonings, French aristocracy, hundreds of deaths, and a secret network of abortionists and fortune tellers, welcome to the tale of Catherine Monvoisin.

6. Halloween Death of Kurt Sova

Five days after disappearing from a house party, the missing boy's body is found – in a location that had already been searched, resulting in a mystery that has never been solved.

7. The Button Man

When four people go missing in less than nine months, in the same area, watched over by a mystery man who spooks people from the shadows, then maybe it's not a coincidence after all.

8. The Bodies of Murder Park

Since 1946, almost 100 bodies have been found in a park in the middle of Baltimore, at least 40 had been murdered by different people, at least 10 remain unsolved.

9. Beachy Head Murder

A young woman disappeared near Beachy Head, a known suicide spot, but nine years later, her body is discovered on top of the cliffs, with links to an infamous serial killer.

10. The One-Legged Man

A criminal fitted with an unbreakable GPS ankle tracker became the prime suspect in a murder, even though the GPS data reported he had never left his home – or at least, not all of him.

11. First Case of Hacking in History

People gathered in anticipation for the first public demo of the wireless telegram system, only for the world's first hacker to tap the signal – and use Morse code to insult the inventor!

12. Soul Eater and the Runaway Devil

A man claiming to be a 300-year-old vampire, and a 12-year-old girl, fell into a forbidden love which left the girl's entire family murdered – a dark tale that concludes with a disturbing twist.

13. Battle of Lanarca Airport

Forced to return with the plane they had hijacked, two assassins and their hostages watched from the windows in shock, as special forces opened fire – on each other.

14. Nude in the Nettles

A strange phone call leads to the discovery of a woman's body on the North York Moors, but for over 40 years, her identity and death remain a mystery, and one of England's oddest unsolved cold cases.

15. Cult of the Black Lords

A female cult leader who taught 'Conscious Development' to fight the Black Lords, was accused of mind control murder, after many of her followers died, and left her everything they owned.

16. Shoe Fetish Slayer

The dark tale of a killer, whose overpowering fetish for women's shoes, led him to abduct and murder his victims while dressed as a woman – before committing unspeakable acts against their corpses.

17. Killings of Templeton Woods

After the first Templeton Woods murder, girls stopped walking the streets alone, after the second, the area became ground zero for Britain's most infamous cold case, with links to the Zodiac Killer.

18. The Real 'Orphan'

Straight out of the Hollywood horror 'Orphan', a loving couple adopt a young girl, only to discover she is an adult, who stands at the end of their bed at night, holding a knife.

19. Case of the Lego Kleptomaniac

A fraudster used an unusual method to illegally purchase Lego sets to sell on eBay, but he didn't need the money, as he was a multi-millionaire vice president of a Silicon Valley software giant.

20. Bumbling Burglar Trapped in Escape Room

A burglar broke into an escape room to rob the place, but when he went to leave, realised he quite literally couldn't escape, so had to call the police to come and rescue him.

The Villisca Axe Murders

In a town known as the pretty place, an entire family were killed by an axeman who had been hiding in their attic waiting for them to go to sleep, in a case that continues to haunt to this day.

The pretty place

Known as the pretty place, Villisca in Montgomery County, Iowa, was once a flourishing midwestern town that became synonymous with one of the state's most infamous unsolved murders.

The early 1900s had brought good fortune to Villisca with over twenty trains a day pulling up to the local station. At the start of the 20th Century, the county was booming and Villisca was enjoying massive success.

But on 10th June 1912, the harmony of the town was replaced with darkness and scattered throughout the lives of those affected. It clouded Villisca in tales of murder and hauntings, that for a century show no signs of lifting.

On an unassuming residential street, sat a quaint, white-framed house with green gardens surrounding it, offering a promise of a good life with solid family values. The area was considered safe, homely, and peaceful.

Strange then, that when residents of Villisca woke that day, they were given the shocking news that eight of their own had been brutally murdered by an axe-wielding maniac. Two adults and six children had been snatched out of the world in a haze of blood and death.

A century later, the murders remain unsolved but the crime has never stopped echoing. The original home has been refurbished and renamed; *The Murder House*, where you can take tours of the location of the murders and see if you can solve the mystery yourself.

The Moore's

The head of the household was local businessman Josiah B. Moore whose family had become relatively well-off across various midwestern states. He married the love of his life Sarah Montgomery just before Christmas in 1899.

Both were active members of the local church and were well-liked in the community. Together, they projected the perfect family life, had four children, and settled into their home in Villisca. Their children were Herman, Katherine, Boyd, and Paul, and were often seen out with their parents.

On Sunday 9th June, the day of the murders, Sarah Moore was helping run the Children's Day Program, at the local Presbyterian Church, an annual event to bring the local community together. The event kicked off at 8pm with all the Moore children taken part.

Also involved were the Stillinger sisters, 12-year-old Lena and eight-year-old Ina. Both girls were born on the large Stillinger family farm just outside of Villisca and were two of nine children raised by their parents, Joseph and Sara Stillinger, who had let them go out for the day.

The plan of action for the two sisters was to go to church in the morning, spend lunch and the afternoon with their grandmother, head to the church event in the evening then make their way back home.

Instead of having them walk home alone, Katherine Moore asked her parents if the sisters could stay the night at their home. Josiah phoned the Stillinger household and let one of the older children know that the two sisters would be sleeping over at their house that night.

The event finished at 9.30pm, and the Moore family, along with the two Stillinger sisters, would have arrived at their home shortly before 10pm. At some point from 10pm to the next morning, all eight of them had been murdered.

Massacre

The Moore's usually began their chores from between 5am to 6am on weekday mornings, so at 7am, their neighbour, Mary Peckham, became concerned as she couldn't see any lights on or hear any noise coming from the home.

She knocked on the door just before 8am and tried to open it but it was still locked from the inside. After letting the Moore's chickens out from their coop, she phoned Ross Moore, Josiah's brother, who arrived quickly.

After a quick scout of the windows, Ross let himself in with a spare set of keys his brother had entrusted to him. When he opened his brother's bedroom door, he found two bodies on the bed. Immediately he charged back to the porch and frantically ordered Mary to call the sheriff.

When the police arrived, they entered the home and found a massacre that would have haunted them until the end of their days. Josiah, 43, and Sarah, 39, were found on their bed, they had been brutally murdered as they slept and their skulls crushed by a heavy object.

Herman, 11, Katherine, 9, Boyd, 7, and Paul, 5, were found in the upstairs bedrooms across the first floor. They too had been attacked in their sleep and their skulls crushed. Downstairs in the guest room they found the bodies of Lena Stillinger, 12, and her sister, Ina, 8.

As word spread, residents of the town descended on the property with some even entering the house due to a lack of control by the local police. A few hours later, the Villisca National Guard arrived to secure the residence and cordon off the crime scene.

Rampage

The murder weapon was an axe that belonged to Josiah, and it was found in the guest room where the sisters were murdered. An investigation of the bodies, as much as was possible in 1912, concluded the eight victims were murdered from between midnight and 5am.

The investigation began to slowly piece together what had gone down in the Moore home. Some bizarre discoveries became clues used to reconstruct the killer's path through the house.

Two cigarette butts were found in the attic which suggested the killer had been hiding there until everyone in the home was asleep. At the foot of Josiah and Sarah's bed was a kerosene lamp, suggested to have been placed there by the killer.

The chimney, which was accessible from the attic, had the wick turned off and was located behind the dresser in the parents' bedroom. It seemed the killer had come down the chimney via the attic and used the kerosene lamp to guide him.

As he stood at the foot of the bed, he raised the axe so quickly he left axe marks on the ceiling above him. Josiah was the first to die and had been savaged by the sharp end of the axe, so viciously that his eyes were missing. Sarah had her skull crushed by the blunt end of the axe as he alternated between the two adults.

Once the parents were dead, he crept upstairs to the children's bedrooms and smashed their heads in as they slept. They were found in a similar state to Sarah, suggesting the blunt end of the axe had been used to murder them.

The killer then went back down to the parents room and used the axe to inflict more damage upon their bodies. It has long remained unclear if the killer knew the Stillinger sisters were in the guest room. If he had been in the attic for the purpose of killing the Moore's then he may not have known about the two sisters.

This theory was backed up by some evidence that suggested 12-year-old Lena was awake and attempted to fend off the killer. Lena had defensive wounds on her arms and her body was found in a different position on the bed to the other victims. Her sister, Ina, was killed as she slept.

Lena was found with her nightgown above her waist, which some researchers took to mean she had been abused. However, if it was the killer's intentions to massacre the Moore family outright then the motive didn't seem to be sexual at all, unless abusing Lena was an opportunistic act.

He never left

After all eight people had been murdered, the killer stayed in the house and closed all the curtains. For those windows that didn't have curtains, he used some of the Moore's clothes to cover them.

He returned to each of the rooms and covered the victim's faces with their bed sheets before returning to the parent's room for a half-hearted attempt to clean the axe. Strangely, a cooking pan of bloody water was found on the kitchen table beside a plate of uneaten food. It seemed likely the killer had sat down to eat after his rampage.

Another piece of evidence was a slab of bacon that was found in the parent's bedroom beside the axe. A second slab was found in an icebox near the kitchen. It could only be assumed that the killer had been eating the bacon while hiding in the attic.

Interestingly, all the doors to the home had been locked from the inside. The killer had left through the attic and eloped from Villisca, never to be seen again.

How he did it wasn't the mystery that echoed across a century, but why he did it and who he was, have tortured cold case investigators for years. However, there were many suspects at the time and many theories have perpetuated online.

Everyone's a suspect

The murders had disrupted the pretty place so much that virtually every person in the town of 2,500 people were a suspect at one point. This led to paranoia and fear among residents that their own neighbours could have been the killers.

Whenever residents went out, they openly carried weapons in full view of local and national press, and the increased police and National Guard presence. Friends were accusing friends and families were in-fighting before huddling together at night in fear of a possible killer among them.

Josiah worked for Frank Jones at the Jones Store, a place that sold tools and landscaping equipment to individuals and businesses. Josiah left in 1908 and set up his own similar business, taking the John Deere tractor franchise with him, which would have been very lucrative at the time.

Though many point to Jones as the killer, the motive wasn't strong enough and he was discounted early on, despite unbased rumours of Moore having an affair with Jones' daughter-in-law.

Another theory suggested that Jones hired Kansas-based drug-addict William Mansfield to kill Moore and his entire family. It was suggested he was also responsible for the murders of his own family two years later – who had been killed with an axe.

Detectives at the time were convinced Mansfield was the killer, not just of the Moore family, but other murders across the region, due to the similarities of the deaths. They arrested and held him pending trial but he was ultimately released due to solid alibis and a lack of evidence.

Murderer Henry Lee Moore (no relation) was considered a suspect after the fact, when he killed his mother and grandmother with an axe in late 1912 in Missouri. Henry Lee has long been connected with other axe murders but there is no solid evidence to suggest he was the killer.

The priest

Two suspects have stood the test of time and are difficult to discount. The first was an English born priest named Reverend George Kelly. He was the travelling minister in the town on the night of the murders and was known to ask young girls to pose for him.

He attended the Children's Day event and left the town on the 5am train the next morning. It was deemed possible, due to the timing of his departure, that he could have been responsible for the murders.

In the weeks after the murders, he wrote letters to the investigation, the Stillinger family, and other people close to the Moore's, to keep in contact and express his sorrow. When investigators spoke to him about the murders, he believed he had witnessed it.

However, it turned out that Kelly was known to have suffered from mental issues, and police questioned his account of what he was supposed to have seen or heard. In 1914, Kelly was arrested for sending pornographic material through the post, and sexually harassing a secretary.

He was committed to a psychiatric institute, which led investigators to believe he was the real killer. In 1917, Kelly was arrested and charged with the Villisca murders. At two separate trials, due to lack of evidence and false confessions, he was acquitted.

There is a big difference in mentality between lusting over young girls and taking an axe to eight people in what was a premediated murder rampage. It is possible that Kelly was responsible but if his motive was to abuse Lena Stillinger or another of the children then killing everyone with an axe seemed very much like overkill.

The killer it seemed was unaware of the Stillinger sisters in the guest room. If Kelly was the killer then he would have known the sisters were at the Children's Day event and left with the Moore's. It seems unlikely he would have left the event to hide out in the attic.

Despite inconsistencies in his story and the nature of his personality, he remains one of the prime suspects in the murders. But there is another, whose tale is even more likely.

The German

Back in 1897, fifteen years before Villisca, a man called Paul Mueller became the prime suspect in the murders of a family in Massachusetts. He had been staying with the family as an employed farmhand on their land. A yearlong manhunt failed to capture Mueller, who was allegedly from Germany.

A book called *The Man on the Train* detailed how Mueller was either arrested for another crime or went into hiding before emerging a few years later to kill again. The authors link Mueller to many axe murders around the same time as the Villisca massacre.

In September and October 1911, three separate families were killed in their own homes by an axe-wielding maniac. The Burnham-Wayne's in Colorado, The Dawson's in Illinois, and the Showman's in Kansas.

Just days prior to the Villisca massacre, Ronald Hudson and his wife were killed by an unidentified axeman in Kansas. All the murders took place on popular train routes and at residences close to train stations, which were easily accessible.

It was then suggested Mueller had returned to Germany, where in 1922, he may have been responsible for the infamous Hinterkaifeck murders – detailed in Bizarre True Crime Volume 2. There, an entire family of six were killed with an axe, on their farm, by someone who had been living in the attic.

Murder house

The pretty house in Villisca sold to various new owners over the years until 1994 when it was purchased by Darwin and Martha Linn of Iowa. They restored the home to how it would have looked at the time of the murders in 1912.

The house was then listed on the National Registrar of Historic Places which meant it was able to open its doors to dark tourists and offer guides around the house. It has long since been known as *The Murder House*.

For just $10 (USD) you can turn up on their open days and take a tour of the house where eight people were brutally murdered. For just over $400, you can book an overnight stay in the house, and the owners will come back for you in the morning! Link in the bibliography.

The house has also become a hotspot for paranormal investigators and psychics. Some recent incidents include sightings of ghosts, lights switching on and off, cold spots in the locations the murders took place, flying objects, and children's voices.

What is certain, is that the walls of the house still protect the identity of the killer who took an axe to eight people. A century later, the case of the Villisca Axe Murders continues to haunt the souls of those who come across it.

Truth Stranger than Fiction

A detective reads a self-published fiction novel and discovers similarities to a real murder three years earlier, along with clues in the book that only the real killer would have known.

Brutal murder

Wroclaw in southwestern Poland is the largest city in the historical region of Silesia with a population of over 1.25million. Sitting on the banks of the River Oder, the area is popular for non-commercial fishing, with many fishermen dangling their rods into the current, hoping for a decent catch.

Murder is considered a rare crime for a city of its size, but on 10th December 2000, a group of fishermen discovered a body on the banks of the river near a weir. It was immediately clear from the condition of the body that murder had washed up on the riverside of Wroclaw.

Police identified the corpse as that of a local businessman named Dariusz Janiszewski who had disappeared four weeks earlier, reported missing by his wife. He was the owner of a small advertising agency in the heart of the city, his business was going from strength to strength, and his disappearance was out of character.

When pathologists examined the body they found he had suffered a particularly brutal death. His hands had been tied behind his back with the same length of rope that weaved around his neck in a noose, in such a way that any movement with his hands would have forced his neck back.

Janiszewski was found with broken bones and a bruised face, the result of a lengthy and sustained beating. The examiners also found signs his limbs had been forcibly stretched to inflict severe pain. On top of all that, he had been starved, tortured, and stabbed to death before being stripped and dumped in the river.

Not a usual day for police in Wroclaw but a case that would result in the most unusual of conclusions. It was a murder that would become synonymous with a work of fiction in which the author would weave clues only known to the killer himself.

The coldest of cold cases

It turned out that Janiszewski had no known enemies, was well-liked within the professional community, and had run a successful business. The motives behind his murder were difficult for police to ascertain, and for the first two years, they came up with nothing.

After a six month investigation, the case went cold and was left unsolved, something that angered Janiszewski's family and friends. But with no evidence to go on, no witnesses, and no way of moving the investigation forward, the police had to temporarily close the case.

In early 2003, a little over two years later, a Polish crime show reconstructed the murder and aired it on national TV. It brought the case into the spotlight but resulted in multiple dead ends.

Reconstructions of crimes on shows such as Crimewatch, though generally lined with good-intentions, tend to result in false witness accounts, exaggerated theories, and a raft of phone calls to the investigating police station that can in some cases cause more problems than solutions.

In the case of the Janiszewski murder, police began receiving emails from all over the world. Various messages came in from South Korea, Indonesia, and Japan, among others, describing the case as the perfect crime and that it would never be solved.

Things quietened again until the Autumn of 2003, when Chief Inspector Jacek Wroblewski took over the cold case file from local police. It was known as the coldest of cold cases, and one the local police were happy to rid themselves of. Jacek was known as Jack Sparrow by his colleagues due to the translation of his Polish name to English, and his propensity to dress-down in the office.

He immediately concluded the murder was a result of someone having a deep grievance against Janiszewski, rather than being a random act of murder or a robbery. As he delved deeper into the files, he began to link things the original investigation had missed.

Bala

Janiszewski's mother had given a statement, that on the day of her son's disappearance, a man had called his advertising business demanding to speak to him. Janiszewski's mother said that she could help him with his requests but the mystery man insisted he specifically wanted Janiszewski to deal with him.

She gave the man her son's mobile number and thought nothing of it until her son went missing. Janiszewski showed up at the office later that morning and said he was meeting the man on the phone in the afternoon. He left the office at 4pm, left his car in the parking lot – and turned up dead four weeks later. It was the only lead Wroblewski had to go on.

Realising that Janiszewski's mobile phone had never been found, he began a search of the serial number of the device and discovered it had been sold on an internet auction site only four days after the body had washed up.

The seller was listed as 'ChrisB', who was in fact a self-published author and photographer named Krystian Bala. Initially, Wroblewski thought it too convenient that a murderer would have listed his victim's phone online on a public site, and so Bala was discounted as a suspect – until Wroblewski looked deeper.

Bala had moved abroad to South-East Asia, penning himself as a travel writer and blogger on the side, which meant he wasn't easy to reach. Wroblewski hunted down a copy of Bala's recently published book named 'Amok'.

Wroblewski found the book to be sadistic, pornographic, and creepy, with a murder of a woman and dark passages of prose. When he compared the real life case to the description of murder in the book, there were shocking similarities.

Amok

'I tightened the noose around her neck.'

This was one of the lines from the book that made Wroblewski sit up and take notice. The main character narrating the story was called Chris, the same name Bala used to sell Janiszewski's phone on the auction site. Already the similarities were mounting.

Bala, it seemed, was a law unto himself and used various philosophies and writings to create his own version of how life should be lived. He boasted about drunken visits to brothels and submissions to temptations of the flesh, both heterosexual and homosexual.

He told friends that he was capable of anything and that he would not live long but live furiously. By 2000, a few months before Janiszewski disappeared, Bala had filed for bankruptcy and ended his marriage.

His wife, Stasia, claimed they had been separated for quite some time, and Bala had taken to travelling as a means of escape, often visiting the United States and Asia, where he was known to have taught English. While he travelled he worked on his book; Amok.

'God, if you only existed, you'd see how sperm looks on blood.'

'I'm a good liar because I believe in the lies myself.'

'I pulled the knife and rope from underneath the bed, as if I were about to begin a children's fairy tale.'

'With my other hand, I stabbed the knife below her left breast. Everything was covered in blood."

The book was self-published in 2003, half a year after he had finished writing it, and three years after Janiszewski's murder.

Murder, he wrote

Wroblewski began to focus on various passages and descriptions in the book as points of interest. Though the main character killed a woman and not a man, the description of the murder was similar, including the noose and the knife.

The character of Chris also sold the knife on an internet auction site a few days after the killing, which mirrored the selling of Janiszewski's phone – a snippet of information that had never been released to the public. Chris also alluded to killing a man who bothered him.

Wroblewski gathered together a group of colleagues to interpret the book page by page. They kept what they were doing quiet and did not speak to Bala or his friends and family. Because Bala was out of the country, they didn't want to spook him before they were certain.

As they went through the book, they discovered similarities to Bala's life, including various early criminal records, relationships, and businesses he had run.

A criminal psychologist who was asked to draw a conclusion on the book, wrote of the main character; *'His way of functioning shows features of psychopathic behaviour. He is testing the limits to see if he can actually carry out his sadistic fantasies. He treats people with disrespect, considers them to be intellectually inferior to himself, uses manipulation to fulfil his own needs, and is determined to satiate his sexual desires in a hedonistic way.'*

The psychologist warned it was common for novelists to have overlaps with their real lives, and that basing an analysis of an author from their fictional character would be incorrect. More importantly, a work of fiction was not evidence at all.

Evidence

Wroblewski used Amok as a road map to a crime and started to link real-world people and descriptions to the fictional world of the book. They found another clue when Bala's buyer account had watched the listing of a book called 'Accidental, Suicidal, or Criminal Hanging.'

In the early Autumn of 2005, Bala returned home and was brought in for questioning by Wroblewski, who was certain that Bala was the killer they were looking for. Bala simply claimed the book was fiction and any similarities to the murder had only been added through his imagination, a coincidence at best.

When questioned on the listing of Janiszewski's phone, he claimed he had bought it in a pawn shop but wasn't sure where, as it had been five years earlier. With nothing solid to hold him on, the police let him go. Bala went straight to the press and claimed the Polish police had kidnapped and beat him while attempting to get a confession.

A short while after, Wroblewski discovered that Bala's passport proved he had been in South Korea, Indonesia, and Japan, when the emails were sent to the Crimewatch-style show in 2003, claiming the murder to be a perfect crime. The passport stamps, along with IP addresses on page views of the murder's appeal page, suggested it was Bala who had sent the emails.

Second novel

But Wroblewski and the investigation needed a motive. Bala going public, though frustrating to the investigation, was also a godsend. Witnesses had started to come forward. A friend of Bala's wife, Stasia, was in a nightclub with her in the Summer of 2000 when she saw Stasia on the dancefloor, dancing with none other than Janiszewski.

Two weeks after the murder, Bala and Stasia were at a bar when a bartender began flirting with Stasia. Bala become angry and threatened to kill the bartender, claiming he had recently killed a man for the exact same reason.

When Wroblewski finally got to interview Bala's former wife, who had refused up until that point to talk anyone, he discovered the motive. Even though they were separated at the time, Stasia claimed that shortly after the nightclub incident, Bala had drunkenly smashed down her door and beat her.

Bala had apparently hired a private detective to watch her and Janiszewski, and discovered they had been having an affair, though none of this has ever been proven. But for Wroblewski, it was motive.

In 2007, Bala was put on trial for the murder of Janiszewski but pleaded not guilty as he believed the evidence was circumstantial at best. Despite no witnesses to Janiszewski's kidnapping and ultimate murder, Bala was found guilty. After a retrial in December 2008, he was found guilty again and sentenced to 25 years in prison.

In prison, Bala is known to be working on a second novel, and with evidence found on his computer, police believe he is tying the book into a second as yet unidentified victim.

'There's never been a book quite like this.' – Bala.

The Uncatchable

A man known as the Greek Robin Hood, went on a 30-year crime spree, gave money to the poor, twice broke out of prison with a helicopter, and broke into prison to rescue his brother – with a tank.

Greek Robin Hood

'Criminals snatch purses from old ladies. Vassilis Paleokostas was on a different level: he is a socially accepted bandit and a hero.' – one of his former cellmates.

Tales of Robin Hood type characters are few and far between but many miss the vital ingredient of actually giving their loot to the poor. Vassilis was and is different, for he is still at large today, earning him the nickname of The Uncatchable.

Vassilis has been arrested and sent to prison multiple times, but on every occasion he has escaped using methods normally seen in a Hollywood movie.

On one occasion, after his brother was imprisoned for helping him, he stole a tank and brazenly drove the giant military vehicle straight into the wall of the prison in order to rescue him.

This is the bizarre tale of the man they call the Greek Robin Hood.

King of the mountains

Vassilis was born in 1966, in the snow-capped village of Moschofyto, around 220 miles North of Athens. At the time, it was a remote cluster of wooden shacks, but now unsurprisingly part of the tourist trail through Greece.

He lived with his father who was a goat herder, and his older brother, Nikos, who he had come to idolise for his strength and resilience to the harsh mountain conditions. In the tough winters, Nikos would carry Vassilis on his shoulders and walk three miles to the local school.

In 1979, the family moved to the town of Trikala, 40 miles to the east, where Nikos left home to work in the burgeoning shipping industry. Vassilis, 13 at the time, worked in a cheese factory during a moment of history when Greece was primed to join the European Union.

But Vassilis wasn't ready for the giant changes to come and felt that working in the factory was tantamount to working as a slave for bosses that didn't appreciate him. As a mountain boy, the only way of living he knew was to live off the land and steal for his family.

Nikos returned from the ships shortly after, and for the next seven years until 1986, Vassilis and Nikos carried out 27 robberies of stores and businesses, mostly stealing VHS recorders and video tapes, something that was a real novelty to a mountain boy in the 1980s.

During their petty crime spree, they were introduced to *The Artist*, Costas Samaras, a self-proclaimed mastermind thief, who kept plans of robberies he intended to pull off in the future. Together they began robbing jewellers and banks.

Their plans intricately involved distraction, blocking doors of police stations, leaving spikes in road for police cars, and more importantly – never keeping all the loot to themselves. Vassilis would give the loot to people from poor communities.

Rather than simply hand it to the needy, he would raise the cost of their services by massive degrees. He would go to a farm and ask for a pig to be killed for meat then leave the farmer one hundred times the asking price, he also handed out large sums of money and loot to homeless people.

The prison and the tank

By 1990, the two brothers and Costas were well known around Greece as wanted robbers, but despite the Greek press vilifying them, the public were warming to their particular brand of crime, specifically giving most of their loot to the poor.

As inflation increased four-fold in as many years, the public needed a hero, and they got one in Vassilis. Nikos was arrested for one of the robberies and sent to prison, but refusing to let him languish inside, Vassilis came up with a plan that solidified his folk tale across Greece.

Vassilis stole a tank from a nearby unsecured military base and drove it through the town towards the prison where his brother was being held. The guards at the prison were made aware of a possible prison break but were none the wiser as to how it would happen.

When reports of a tank were seen nearby, they had no idea it was headed towards them. Suddenly, the tank breached the prison's perimeter fence, sped up, and crashed through the thick walls.

As the alarms went off, and the prison erupted in chaos, the guards were called to action. The tank became trapped within the walls of the prison and Vassilis was arrested and put in a cell close to his brother.

But one has to wonder if that was the plan all along, because a few months later, as 1991 came around and Bush began his Iraq war campaign, the brothers escaped. They tied bed sheets together and climbed out of the window.

Legendary robbery

The brothers and Costas became public enemy number one in the country, except the public didn't see them as the enemy at all. In 1992, they pulled off the largest cash robbery in Greek history, at Meteora, a mountainous region with famous rocky outcrops topped with ancient monasteries.

They stole a local car, walked into the only bank in the town, and stole 125 million drachmas, (approximately 400,000 GBP in cash). As they led police on a wild goose chase around the region, they handed out blocks of cash to passing pedestrians and locals.

Vassilis returned the stolen car to the local owner in the middle of the night, freshly polished, cleaned, and with a full tank of gas – along with a wedge of cash and a thank you note stuffed into the glove box.

The bandits continued with the robberies, and some kidnappings of wealthy individuals, until 1999 when Vassilis was arrested after crashing a car into a tree on the side of the road. He was sentenced to 25 years at the Corfu prison, an imposing building nestled on the top of a hill.

Inside the prison, he convinced the guards and chaplain to provide the other prisoners with new shoes and a better quality of life. When guards found a detailed plan to escape Corfu prison, involving tunnels, and sewers, Vassilis was sent to the maximum security Korydallos prison near Athens.

Prison escape

In 2006, after one year in Korydallos, Vassilis had already colluded with other prisoners for a breakout but someone else had other ideas. Unknown to Vassilis at the time, Niko wanted to return the favour for the attempted breakout with the tank.

A tour helicopter took off from Athens in the early evening on 4th June 2006, unfortunately for the pilot, Nikos was the passenger. He told the pilot the sight-seeing trip was over and ordered him to land at Korydallos prison.

The pilot informed the guards that the passenger had bombs and was willing to use them unless Vassilis was released to them. Vassilis took his cellmate with him, an Albanian assassin named Alket Rizai, they thanked the guards for their hospitality and the helicopter flew away to land in cemetery north of Athens.

Nikos and Costas were captured shortly after but Vassilis and Rizai escaped and promised to continue taking from the rich to give to the poor. In 2008, he and Rizai kidnapped a billionaire who had belittled Greek's working class by telling them to work harder and longer.

After putting up a ransom of 12 million euros, they were captured after being tracked with the money that was delivered for the billionaire. Swat burst through the door where they were staying and found the pair drinking moonshine and watching a DVD.

At Vassilis and Rizai's trial in 2009, thousands of people protested against the establishment and requested Vassilis be released, as they believed he had done more to help the people of Greece than the government had.

Escape to victory

Rizai had a girlfriend named Soula Mitropia, who hugged him in the courtroom as he was led away with Vassilis. Unbeknownst to the watching guards and lawyers, she slipped a mysterious gold watch into his pocket.

On 22nd February 2009, Rizai and Vassilis were back in Korydallos prison, as a holding location for the trial, on what seemed like an ordinary day. Until guards heard the sound of a helicopter approaching from the city.

It turned out, the mysterious watch was a tiny mobile phone. Mitropia phoned Rizai and told him to get ready. The plan was to use the exercise timetable of the prison to ensure both Rizai and Vassilis were outside.

Mitropia threatened another unsuspecting tour helicopter pilot with a grenade and a machine gun, and they hovered above the exercise area. She threw a rope ladder down, and both men climbed into the helicopter which made its getaway in front of the guards, and journalists who were camped on the prison's doorsteps.

The prisoners inside Korydallos were heard cheering at yet another escape but three guards stormed to the top of the prison building and opened fire, hitting the helicopter's fuel tank. Greek television was interrupted by live images of the daring rescue as pedestrians filmed on their phones.

The Phantom

The helicopter managed to land safely, and Vassilis went on the run again, with Rizai and Mitropia. Vassilis was never seen again. Even the CIA became involved and have intelligence officers permanently camped in Greece, with Vassilis as their number one target.

Rizai and Mitropia, who became known as the blonde Lara Croft, were arrested after another robbery in 2009. But Vassilis has never been caught and continues to evade capture.

Even to this day, despite sightings and dramatic police chases through mountainous regions, he remains a fugitive. But the thefts continue, and the poorest in Greece are being left packages of money at the door in the middle of the night.

From 2010, due to the financial crash of the country and other problems, the country has faced numerous riots and massive unemployment. All over Greece, you can find graffiti and posters proclaiming Vassilis to be a hero of the people.

The public believe he is being protected by monks in the mountains, and that he leaves every now and again to rob the rich and give to the poor. He is now known as *The Phantom*.

'If you steal something small you are a petty thief, but if you steal millions you are a gentleman of society.' - Greek Proverb

Truman Library Robbery

Thieves broke into the Presidential Library and stole a selection of ceremonial swords and daggers worth over $1million – in under 45 seconds – leading to theories the items were stolen to order.

Presidential Library

In July 2021, the Harry S. Truman Presidential Library and Museum in Independence, Missouri, reopened after a two-year-long, $25million renovation that provided a new museum entrance and redesigned inner spaces.

This included a permanent exhibition in celebration of the 75th anniversary of Truman's ascension to the presidency. However, there are some items from one of the displays at least, that are notably missing.

On a snowy day in March 1978, thieves broke into the library and stole a collection of swords and daggers worth $1million at the time. The ceremonial items were gifted to President Truman by the Saudi Crown Prince Saud and the Shah of Iran, on one of their visits.

What is curious about the robbery is that the thieves knew exactly what they were going for, where the security guards would be, and the speed of the theft itself. For over 40 years, no trace of the items have ever been found – and no one has ever been linked.

Possible decoy

On 24th March, at 6.20am, security guard Thomas Williams was on duty at his guard station, coming to the end of his night shift. Before the changeover, he relaxed a little bit more, knowing he would shortly be going home for some much-needed rest.

Guarding the museum and library was not a difficult job and the most action Thomas had seen until that point was ordering the groups of school children to stay away from some of the exhibits. Maintenance man Neil Morris, who had arrived earlier in the morning, was chatting with Thomas at the guard station.

As they sought to solve the world's problems through random chat, something caught their eye. A mysterious woman was walking nearby, unusually dressed for such a cold morning. She held their attention for many minutes, and some have come to believe she may have been a decoy.

Ten minutes later, Thomas and Neil noticed a black Oldsmobile park across the street where the same woman got out of the car, walked around the vehicle, and then drove off. At that moment, the alarm went off and Thomas realised that a robbery was in progress.

45 seconds

At 6.30am, two unidentified men had calmly walked up to the front entrance of the library and brazenly smashed the window of the front door. They charged straight to the display unit containing the jewel-encrusted swords and daggers and broke the glass of the display.

At that point, Thomas was only 100 feet away, running along the main corridor from the north to the south side of the library, in a breathless attempt to stop the thieves in their tracks.

He arrived at the display and saw the glass had been smashed, then he heard chains on the door closest to him and tried to open it. The thieves had chained the inner door from the other side, stopping Thomas from following them, something which would have been planned out beforehand.

The chaining of the door allowed the thieves to return through the broken glass of the front entrance and off into the darkness of the early morning, long before the dawn rose on one of the most brazen robberies the state of Missouri had ever seen.

Interesting then, that the case is rarely spoken about, nor detailed elsewhere aside from various appeals seeking new information. It was claimed the robbery had lasted just 45 seconds and the only evidence police had were two footprints in the snow that led nowhere.

Clutching at straws

Carol Burnett was an employee at the library and arrived at her workplace that morning to be met with scores of police and FBI agents. Her desk was just across the room from the swords and daggers display, and she would often joke that the jewels on the weapons were the best thing in the building.

One of the small broken pieces of glass had slid across the floor to her desk, and for some reason, Burnett took the piece of glass home with her, where it remains in storage to this day, as a souvenir. Later she was interviewed by the FBI and shown mugshots but she recognised no one.

It appeared that from the very beginning, the FBI were clutching at straws, and could only offer conjecture as to who had been responsible. Aside from the time the robbery had taken place, the speed, the efficiency, and the possible female decoy, they wasn't much to go on.

Six months after the robbery, a news report suggested a theory that, *'somewhere in the United States, a collector, clad in a smoking jacket and sipping an expensive liqueur, sits in a vault deep in the bowels of his mansion and smiles. On a wall in front of him is the object of his satisfaction. It is an exclusive array of three swords and two daggers worth nearly $1 million.'*

Another theory suggested the thieves would have melted down the swords and daggers to remove the jewels, which by themselves would have been worth in the region of $250,000 in 1978. The jewels, which were only archived in document form, could then have been sold on and remade into various jewellery items.

Lost swords

The FBI later claimed there were certain collectors in the world who would pay an astonishing amount of money for an item to be stolen if they strongly desired it for their collection. However, if the jewels were cut up then the FBI admitted they would be impossible to trace.

Three weeks before the Truman Library robbery, in February of 1978, some thieves had attempted to break into the library but at a different time. The security guard on duty that day was able to scare them off. It is possible they were the same thieves testing the library's security system before going all in on the morning of the robbery.

In 1962, a collection of rare coins were stolen from the Truman Library, worth over $50,000. Maybe the 1978 robbers saw the library as a weak spot and knew it was possible to get away with it. Or maybe they did steal the swords to order, as they had no intention of going after any of the other displays.

One of the more interesting aspects of the case is that people on the streets were not talking about it. The police said that criminals and informants they were aware of kept silent on the matter, because either they didn't know anything or they were keeping their lips sealed.

In March 2021, the FBI put up a reward of $10,000 for information leading to the return of the swords and daggers, a token reminder they have never given up. However, with the statute of limitations now long passed, it seems the thieves may have got away with the ultimate robbery.

Black Mass of the Fortune Teller

Black magic, witchcraft, poisonings, French aristocracy, hundreds of deaths, and a secret network of abortionists and fortune tellers, welcome to the tale of Catherine Monvoisin.

Evil fortune tellers

When it comes to body count, mystery, and utter bizarreness, the tale of Catherine Monvoisin will chill you to the white of your bones.

Born in 1640 France, 26 years after Elizabeth Bathory's demise at Castle Csejte, Catherine Monvoisin would become known across the city of Paris, and France, by her moniker of La Voisin. She plied her wares in the realm of fortune telling and was alleged to have been an advocate and practitioner of black magic.

Over time, she became the head of a large network of fortune tellers who provided macabre services to the French aristocracy and other wealthy people. These services included poisoning, abortion, arranging black masses, and the promotion and selling of dangerous aphrodisiacs.

Her crimes and those around her would eventually result in a major scandal in France that became known as the Affair of the Poisons during the reign of King Louis XIV. In the scandal, detailed in this tale, members of the aristocracy were charged with poisoning and witchcraft.

La Voisin became a central figure in the scandal due to her large network of evil fortune tellers. When details of the scandal were released over the passage of time, the public learned that La Voisin and her network had commissioned black magic rituals and poisonings said to have killed between 1,000 and 2,500 people.

Rising popularity

When Catherine was a young woman, she married a jeweller and silk merchant named Antoine Monvoisin. Antoine's business went bust shortly after and he applied for bankruptcy. To support the family, Catherine, who was also a midwife at the time, turned to her one true passion to keep the bills paid.

Since the age of nine, she believed God had imbibed her with the power to heal others, through chiromancy and face-reading. From the early 1660s she turned to fortune telling as a way to bring in the money, but before she knew it, she was becoming one of the most popular fortune tellers in Paris.

As her spiritual abilities gained admiration across the region, she garnered the attention of some members of the French aristocracy and other wealthy people, who at the time believed in a fortune teller's ability to heal.

In 1664, she purchased an expensive crimson red velvet robe, said to have been embroidered with images of eagles in golden thread. As she developed her image as one of France's lead fortune tellers, she began to increase her client base rapidly.

From the mid-1660s, Catherine was supporting a family of six, including her children, her husband, and her mother. Though Antoine had become second-fiddle to his wife's illustrious career path. Catherine abused his position of trust and took at least six lovers while they were together.

Her lovers included an executioner, an alchemist, an architect, and a magician named Adam Lesage.

Lesage was so besotted with Catherine, he attempted to coerce her into killing Antoine so he could have her all to himself. It is claimed she changed her mind at the last minute.

Convinced of her powers

In 1665, a priest from the Saint Vincent de Paul's Order questioned Catherine's abilities in public, but not one to back down, she held a lecture in front of professors at Sorbonne University to explain how her gifts worked.

The professors were so convinced of her powers that they spread the word among their peers, and yet again, Catherine's clientele increased, to the point that she became a well-known figure in the King's court.

Important people began asking for advice and how to perform secret medical procedures, and it was then that things went a little bit more macabre.

Enemies were beginning to rise on all sides, including many new fortune tellers, people wary of her powers, and some members of the aristocracy who believed what she was doing was tantamount to witchcraft.

Then, Catherine, now known as La Voisin, learned that many people who came to see her wished another person to be dead. Usually this had come out of a broken heart or straying lover, and the desired outcome was the death of a spouse or enemy.

Abortions and potions

La Voisin was also taking payments to carry out abortions in secret, which were illegal back then, as a side project to bring in more money for the family. It was this veil of secrecy surrounding her services that would lead to more people in power coming to her for help.

Realising she couldn't feed everyone's desires, she built a network of abortion providers who she could refer clients to on a referral fee basis. Which meant that when one member of her network was sent a client who wanted an abortion, La Voisin would keep a percentage of the fee – and get richer.

It was claimed the underground abortion industry was so large in 17th Century France, that many of the foetuses were burned in a furnace and buried in La Voisin's garden. Though when it came to the trial, the abortion side of the story took a back seat to the poisonings.

To capitalise on people's desire to heal, kill, and tread between the line of right and wrong, she expanded her services to include the selling of potions and powders. On top of her fortune telling, she began to sell poisons to her clients.

Some of the potions contained the bones of toads, powdered teeth, iron dust, human blood, human ashes, and an aphrodisiac known as Lytta Vesicatoria, or more commonly; Spanish Fly.

She would put her clients through a gradual program of church visits to praise a particular saint, and when that didn't work, which it undoubtedly didn't, then she would move onto amulets, magic objects, and then ultimately the poisons.

By this point she was known to be performing black masses, in which she used a woman's body as a living altar for spirits to be worshipped. For a large fee, she allowed her client to pray to Satan for their wishes or desires to be made true.

On those occasions, she would arrange for a woman to be laid or sat at an altar. There, she would place a bowl on the woman, hold a baby above the bowl, and sacrifice the baby so that its blood could flow freely into the bowl. It is suspected the babies were stillborn or had already died from natural causes, rather than being alive.

King's mistress

Poisoning in the 17th Century was an art form, a novelty to come out of the alchemist's lab. Just two decades before La Voisin, an Italian poisoner named Giulia Tofana had perfected the art of combining various ingredients. Yet, La Voisin was the one to perfect it for criminal purposes.

As her abortion network grew in size, La Voisin realised she could supply her poisons to the same network alongside a newly developed network of fortune tellers she had been overseeing. So, as the clients grew, more and more poisonings were taking place – and people were dying across the city.

In 1667, La Voison received a visit from Claude de Vin des Oeillets, who was a companion and confidant to

Madame de Montespan, a mistress of King Louis XIV. Having heard of La Voisin's incredible powers, Montespan recruited her to help win the love of King Louis.

At a large mansion, on the ancient streets of Paris, La Voison and other magicians held a secret black mass for Montespan while she prayed to win the love of the King. The same year, Montespan became the official mistress of the King and put her good fortune down to La Voison.

Montespan then sought La Voison's special skills whenever a problem occurred both in her personal and professional life. This solidified La Voison's position among the French aristocracy for the next six years.

In 1673, Montespan was suspicious the King was cheating on her with another mistress and employed the services of La Voison to perform multiple black masses. At least one of the black masses involved Montespan as the female altar herself.

An engraving in 1895 by Henry de Malvost shows a nude Montespan on the altar having a baby's blood splashed on to her, with La Voison standing nearby. La Voisin provided aphrodisiacs to Montespan so she could poison the King with it.

In 1679, the King fell into a relationship with Angélique de Fontanges. Enraged, Montespan begged La Voison to kill King Louis, and she eventually agreed. La Voison recruited some of her own closest confidants and they came up with a plan.

They decided to poison a petition which would be delivered to the King himself and placed into his hands where the poison would be absorbed by his skin.

Exterminate the network

In March of 1679, La Voison went to the royal court to deliver the petition but failed to get it past the other petitioners. She returned home and had it burned then tried to work out another plan to kill the King.

But her past was catching up to her and rumours of a secret network of witches and poisoners were already rampant among the French public. Just three years earlier, the King's sister-in-law, Duchesse d'Orléans, was suspected to have been poisoned to death.

At her funeral, a riot had taken place where the public were accusing witches of abducting their children for sacrifice in black masses. At the same time, priests and churches were warning the royal court and police that a huge number of people were confessing to poisoning others.

A day after visiting the royal court, La Voison was arrested outside of Notre Dame after a meeting to decide how to kill the King. Hearing about the secret network of poisoners, King Louis issued an order to exterminate the network throughout the city and country.

Up until December 1679, many involved in La Voison's network were arrested, including her own daughter, and the magicians involved in the black masses. The King issued another order giving permission for the use of torture to interrogate the prisoners.

Other high-ranking officials of the aristocracy hushed the order to torture La Voison in case she revealed too many names of people involved. Yet, La Voison knew she had been caught and eventually confessed to having sold poison and black magic services to people within the royal court.

Affair of the Poisons

La Voison was found guilty of witchcraft and sentenced to death by burning. Despite being tortured from her sentencing to execution, she refused to name the people within the Royal Court. On 22nd February 1680, La Voison was strapped to the stake and burned alive.

In July 1680, La Voison's daughter confessed there was a plan in place to poison the King, which had been arranged by people close to the King, including Montespan. The King was outraged that members of the royal court were involved. He closed the investigation and shut down the court where the trials were taking place.

The King signed a royal order known as a 'lettre de cachet' which was an order to enforce a judgement that could not be appealed. It fundamentally removed all of the suspects and prisoners involved in the poisoning case out of the public judicial system and into secrecy.

Many, including La Voison's daughter, were secretly sentenced to perpetual imprisonment in fortresses around the country until their deaths. The commanders of the fortresses were ordered to torture them if they were about to reveal the names of people involved.

Montespan was not publicly disgraced and retired somewhat gracefully to the Filles de Saint-Joseph convent, in the rue Saint-Dominique. Thankful for her departure, the King made her father the governor of Paris. Little justice it seemed for the woman who wanted the King dead.

Other suspects and prisoners escaped the King's order due to the power they still wielded among their peers. Some were banished from Paris and others fled into exile.

The court set up to put witches on trial was abandoned by the King in 1682, as he couldn't risk a public scandal. Over the course of the Affairs of the Poisons, 218 suspects had been arrested, with another 200 unidentified. Out of those, 36 were executed for poisoning or witchcraft. Details of the trial were eventually released as the passage of time went by.

In a book called *Sex with Kings*, by Eleanor Herman, it is claimed police uncovered the remains of 2,500 infants in La Voisin's garden. The size of La Voison's poison network was alleged to have killed at least 1,000 people. Reports from priests and other statements at the time seem to imply this was a conservative figure.

La Voison will forever be connected with the reign of King Louis XIV, in a moment of history that still defies belief to this day.

Halloween Death of Kurt Sova

Five days after disappearing from a house party, the missing boy's body is found – in a location that had already been searched, resulting in a mystery that has never been solved.

Samhain

For many teenagers, Halloween is a big deal. It's a time to meet with friends, attend parties, dress up, and chill-out away from the prying eyes of parents. For the past 2,000 years, since the ancient Celt festival of Samhain, humans have celebrated Halloween.

Celts believed that on the night before the New Year, seen as 1st November, the boundary between the worlds of the living and the dead became blurred. Traditionally, the day marked the end of the summer harvest and the beginning of the winter, a time of year that was linked with human death.

On Friday 23rd October 1981, in Ohio, Cleveland, 17-year-old Kurt Sova left his parents' house in the mid-afternoon and met up with a friend who suggested they go to a Halloween party at a residence in the town.

Five days later, on Wednesday 28th October, three young boys were exploring a ravine on Harvard Street, when they found Kurt's body. It was located less than 500 metres from where the party had taken place.

The night he never came home

Kurt lived with his parents in Newburgh Heights and was the youngest of four brothers. He was close to his family and wouldn't go too far without letting them know where he was. His mother, Dorothy, later stated that he was never in trouble and it was unusual for him to stay out overnight.

On the morning of Saturday 24th, Kurt's parents became concerned as he had not returned home or been in contact with them. Dorothy contacted his friends throughout the day but no one could confirm where Kurt was.

She picked up rumours of a Halloween party that Kurt may have attended and she located the duplex residence and made her way there to see if the owner, Susan, had seen her son. A friend of Susan's answered the door and said she was out babysitting.

Dorothy gave the friend her number and asked Susan to call her. Kurt's parents spent the Sunday plastering missing person flyers around the area in the hope that someone had seen Kurt and could let them know he was safe.

Later that night, Dorothy received a phone call from Susan, who claimed that she never had a Halloween party at the house and had not seen Kurt at all. Suspecting something was amiss, Kurt was officially reported missing.

Everclear

When police became involved, a timeline of the party began to emerge, but with it, confusion and questions. A pizza delivery business confirmed they had sent an order to the duplex, and the driver confirmed there was a party taking place.

When Susan was confronted, she admitted to the Halloween party and that Kurt had been there. She told police that most of the partygoers were from

Detroit, 180 miles away, and that Kurt didn't know many people at the party.

Police quickly tracked down many of the revellers who were at the party and questioned them about Kurt's attendance and appearance. Many claimed to have seen him consuming a powerful alcoholic drink called Everclear.

It is an American grain spirit sold in bottles that contain between 60% to 95% (120-190 U.S. proof) alcohol. It is generally viewed as an unfinished undiluted ingredient that can be mixed with water to make vodka. Over the years, Everclear has developed a notorious reputation among partygoers.

Kurt's parents were shocked that he would be drinking such a powerful spirit straight from the bottle, though they were aware he was consuming normal-level alcohol drinks when out with friends. Perhaps due its reputation and the fact he didn't know many people, he was looking to increase his social standing with fellow revellers.

At some point during the evening, Kurt's friend who had invited him to the party, walked Kurt outside to get some fresh air as he had become overly drunk. As it was a cold October night, the friend went back in to get Kurt's jacket. When he returned to hand him his jacket, Kurt had vanished.

Lies of the unknown

Susan later told Dorothy it was possible Kurt had slept on a small bed in her basement that night. Enraged by the misdirection he was feeling, Kurt's father, Ken, entered Susan's property and searched her basement. There was no sign of Kurt or his belongings but the bed had been slept in. It is possible that Susan had also been drunk, seen someone else on the bed and later believed it to be Kurt.

Dorothy had put a flyer up in a local record shop, and the owner contacted her saying a man had come in two days after and had a weird conversation with him. The man told the owner; *'you might as well take it down as he's gonna be found dead in two days, and nobody's going to know how he died.'*

The statement from the record shop owner came after the body was found, so it seemed likely that the conversation was taken differently. Upon seeing a missing person poster, it can be a common response for someone to believe the missing person is already dead. Some people voice their opinions, and maybe the record shop owner elaborated on the conversation to fit the later narrative.

One of Kurt's schoolmates, Franco, had apparently seen Kurt on Monday 26th October. Franco claimed to have been going for a job interview when he saw Kurt walking towards an unidentified van. He said Kurt was jubilant and happy. Franco didn't recognise the van as being local and didn't know at the time that Kurt had been reported missing.

But if that was Kurt on the Monday, then he must have known that his parents were looking for him and that his friends had been contacted by his mother over the previous two days. It seems unlikely he would just be wandering around.

Were lies being told to cover up the truth or had Kurt genuinely disappeared under mysterious circumstances?

Unusual details

On Wednesday 28th October, after the three little boys found Kurt's body in the ravine, police descended on the area and a possible homicide investigation began. The body was found less than 500 metres from where the party had taken place.

A previous search of the area had already been undertaken and no sign of Kurt's body had been found near the ravine in the three days following the disappearance. Ken himself had searched the ravine as well in great detail and there had been no sign of a body.

An investigation learned there were no indications of an assault and no major injuries suggesting Kurt had been beaten. Curiously, police failed to locate his right shoe. An autopsy discovered that Kurt had been deceased for between 24 and 36 hours, which meant he had died at least three days after the party.

Despite the inconsistencies, Kurt's death was listed as 'probable death by natural causes'. However, his family believed Kurt had died on the 23rd, the night of the party, and that someone knew exactly what had happened that night.

Kurt's parents and two of his brothers have since passed away but the truth of what happened was still begging to come out. In 2020, an innovative event took place at CrimeCon Chicago, where hundreds of volunteer web sleuths and experts were able to look at the details of the crime and see if they could solve it using crowdsourcing and fresh eyes.

Though the results were inconclusive, it seemed to focus on the people at the party. Experts claimed that it may already be too late, as since 40 years had passed, people had begun to forget the minor details, and any lies told may have been exaggerated to the point of being confused over time.

Alcoholic poisoning

It is possible that Susan and some others had lied to cover up the truth. Perhaps Kurt had drunk so much Everclear, he had succumbed to alcoholic poisoning and passed out. Susan and some friends could have put him on the basement bed to sleep it off.

Maybe the poisoning was so severe that he fell into a coma and could not be woken. The people who knew about it, didn't know what to do and panicked, telling lies to say he had left the party.

When he eventually died three days after the party, they placed his body into the ravine to look like an accident, not realising an autopsy would reveal the time of death – or that it had already been searched.

It's also possible that Kurt attempted to stagger home by himself, fell into the ravine, succumbed to the cold, and fell into a coma before dying from the elements at the location he fell. Not finding the body beforehand could have been a massive oversight.

The case was embedded in true crime history, when three months later, in the very same town, a 13-year-old boy named Eugene Kvet was found dead in the same ravine – with his right shoe missing. An autopsy put Eugene's death as accidental, suggesting he too had fallen into the ravine.

Whether Kurt's death was a murder, a cover-up, or an accident – and despite many thousands of people poring over details of the case – it seems the tale may have ended with Kurt himself.

The Button Man

When four people go missing in less than nine months, in the same area, watched over by a mystery man who spooks people from the shadows, then maybe it's not a coincidence after all.

Mysterious bushman

In Australia, an estimated 38,000 people go missing every year but around 98% are found alive and well for a multitude of reasons. That still means approximately 750 people are never found, most having ventured off into the wilderness of the bush or the high country.

Some of the 'never found' may have started a new life somewhere, while others could have been involved an accident and were never discovered. Some meet the unfortunate fate of wandering into the vast landscapes of the country and succumbing to the natural world.

Non-Australians don't often think of the country as having mountainous regions but the Victoria Alpine Park is full of high peaks and treacherous valleys. Most of the region is so vast and rugged, it makes the Scottish Highlands look like the beaches of California.

The sprawling Alpine National Park is located in the Central Highlands and Alpine region of Victoria, sometimes known as the Australian Alps. It's no surprise that people get themselves into trouble but almost all are rescued due to the impressive search and rescue infrastructure in the region.

Between 2019 and 2020, four people disappeared within a 37-mile radius located in the Wonnangatta Valley and have never been found, despite massive search and rescue operations, using professional and volunteer teams.

Stories have started to emerge of a mysterious bushman known only as the Button Man, who may be responsible for people going missing in the mountains – and their deaths.

No trace

The Wonnangatta Valley sits in-between the two ski resorts of Mount Buller and Mount Hotham, and for most people, it can only be accessed by a four-wheel drive vehicle. Known to be impassable in the Winter, it attracts a wide range of hikers, skiers, and climbers.

In July 2019, Conrad Whitlock drove into the valley, left his white BMW on the side of Mount Buller Road and went for a hike on Mount Buller. No trace of him has ever been found.

In October of the same year, experienced hiker and climber Niels Becker was on a five-day solo trip in the Alpine Park, that he had been planning for months. Well-equipped and versed in the landscape, it was a surprise when he failed to contact family afterwards.

When he was reported missing, over 70 people searched for Niels but found no trace of him. A police official suggested he may have been the victim of foul-play. It was considered rare not to find a body near the valley. After the Winter, a body could appear out of the thaw, but Niels was never found.

Vanished

Then in March 2020, Russell Hill and Carol Clay disappeared from their campsite in the Wonnangatta Valley, at a location called Dry River Track. Russell was familiar with the area as he had worked as a logging contractor there many years before.

Though Russell was married at the time, he was having an affair with Carol, who he had picked up from her home and they secretly went on a trip to Wonnangatta. After the disappearance was reported, the family learned that Carol had gone away with him on many a 'solo' trip.

After confirming radio transmission issues, Russell failed to check in with a local radio club and they reported him missing on the 23rd of March. Four days later, their campsite was found by search and rescue, and the vehicle they had used to get there had been set on fire.

What seemed like a case of two adulterous lovers wishing to elope, soon became a mystery. Their phones, banks accounts, and social security numbers were never used again, and it remained a mystery why their camp and vehicle had been set alight. Both Russell and Carol, despite the affair, had good jobs, families, and large social networks.

Russell was known to fly a drone whenever he visited the valley, and his drone had a camera attached to it. A friend of Russell's claimed that in 2019, near the same area, they'd had an encounter with the mystery Button Man who was angry at them for using the drone. He ordered them to leave their camp the next day, which they did.

Before the Australian Winter set in, search and rescue scoured the valley and nearby regions but no trace of Russell or Carol were ever found and no tracks suggested they had gone into the mountains. Many believed they were the victims of foul play – and only one suspect came to mind.

The Button Man

Even before the stories of the missing emerged, locals were talking about a hardened expert bushman who would disappear into the mountains for months at a time. They called him the Button Man, as he would use deer antlers to make buttons and plugs for his ear piercings.

Though no-one knew his real name, he was occasionally seen camped on the side of a remote mountain, at a particular spot that would allow him to see anyone approaching through the valley. Snares and animal traps were found near to where he was supposed to have camped, along with spears that aborigines had used for generations before.

Tourists in the area would report to locals they had seen the Button Man approach them at their campsites in the middle of the night. Said to be aged between 50 and 70, he creeps up on them like a ghost out of the darkness, with short grey hair and a dark jacket.

He would ask the tourists why they were camping in his area and what they were doing near his camp in the middle of the night. He didn't speak about anything else and persisted with the questions before spritely making his way back up the mountain.

Many of the tourists felt threatened by the Button Man, even though he hadn't displayed any physical violence or threats to them. They would later refer to the encounters as genuinely scary.

One experienced hiker was quoted in local press as saying the man had a *'thousand-meter stare that made the hairs on the back of your neck stand up.*' Another claimed to have returned home from the valley to find there was a photo of himself sleeping in his tent – on his own camera.

A hiker had once gone camping in the valley and fell asleep in his tent in complete silence. When he awoke in the early hours of the morning, he found the Button Man camping next to him, just feet away. He described the experience as '*spooky*'.

Hunting the hunters

When police began getting reports of the Button Man terrorising tourists in the valley, they took it upon themselves to hunt him down and find out what was going on. After the thaw, search and rescue police hiked into the valley and up to the mountain where the Button Man was known to camp.

They didn't quite know what to expect but they found the mystery man watching them come up from the mountain track. He calmly told them he had seen a lot of things in the valley but couldn't help them further, though he suspected he had seen Niels Becker hike past his camp in 2019.

He told police he enjoyed watching people, especially hikers who were coming through the valley, and took great pleasure in '*hunting the hunters*'. With no evidence to arrest him for anything, they told him he couldn't camp illegally, then hiked back down the mountain.

Is the Button Man the same person who approached people from the darkness or is there someone else out there in the Wonnangatta Valley? Could the Button Man be someone at one with nature, protecting his patch from messy tourists, or is he truly connected with the disappearances?

For someone that supposedly watches hikers all day long, it would be unusual if he didn't at least know what happened to some of them. It could be a massive coincidence or unfortunate luck that the disappearances happened so close together. But with bizarre evidence left at the scene of the Russell and Carol campsite, it seems something else is afoot.

Though some people believe the Button Man is a myth told by tourists to spook each other around the campfire, it remains clear the police once spoke to the real Button Man, and he was the last person to see one of the missing alive.

The Bodies of Murder Park

Since 1946, almost 100 bodies have been found in a park in the middle of Baltimore, at least 40 had been murdered by different people, at least 10 remain unsolved.

Killing fields

True crime is rife with tales of serial killer dumping grounds, most famously the Texas Killing Fields - and anywhere Pedro Lopez buried clusters of his 300+ victims. In fact some serial killers tend to bury their victims close to each other.

The Moors Murderers, Ian Brady and Myra Hindley, buried some of their victims on Saddleworth Moor in England. The two macabre lovers would then take days out to have a picnic on top of the burial sites in full view of passing walkers, as Brady liked to feel ownership of the bodies.

Killing fields tend to be in remote areas, partly to prevent discovery of the bodies, with killers using that time for evidence to minimise. But there is one location rarely talked about as it seldom pops up on serial killer lists, despite Reginald Vernon Oates having left four bodies in the area.

Leakin Park in Baltimore, Maryland, sits between two high-crime neighbourhoods, though a walk through the park's wooded areas and green pathways seem a world away. It's set on over 1,200 acres, with sports fields, miniature trains, and trails for hiking and biking.

But peer beyond the treeline to the secluded areas off the beaten track, and you'll find a dark history of crime, murder, bodies, and links to a suspected unidentified serial killer.

Leakin Park

Baltimore has a population of between 585,000 (city limits) to 2.8million (metro area), and an average of 250 people are murdered in the city every single year. The lowest since records began was 177 in 1977, and the highest was 353 in 1993. In 2019, 348 people were murdered in Baltimore.

In fact, in cities not at war and with populations of more than 300,000, Baltimore has the 11th highest murder rate in the world, and the second highest rate in the United States, behind St. Louis, Missouri, coming in at number nine.

It's no wonder that Leakin Park has become synonymous with death and has become known to local's as Murder Park. Since 1946, at least 83 bodies have been found in and around Leakin Park, Maryland. Of those, 38 were murder victims, with the most recent discovered in June 2021.

The bodies found in the park belong to both males and females and from ages as young as a baby to elderly people. Not much connects the murder victims despite being found in the park.

Some victims were killed by their own children, others by their husbands and wives, while some were the victim of a serial killer. One known and one unknown.

Oates

The 1970s and 1980s were notorious for serial killers, for many cultural, environmental, and societal reasons, but the rise of the serial killer had begun in the 1960s. Born in 1950, Reginald Oates would go on to kill four young boys over two days in April, 1968. Their bodies were dumped in Leakin Park.

Baltimore-born and raised, Oates was racially abused at school and accused of minor crimes he didn't commit. Three years before the murders, aged 15, he was accused of attempting to rob another student and ultimately sentenced to two years in juvenile prison, despite only circumstantial evidence.

There, he was raped and beaten by other prisoners, leading to a deterioration of his mental health, along with physical scars received as a brutal reminder of his life there. When he was released, he became a waste collector and involved himself in the Christian church, but the scars were burning deep.

On 17th April 1968, Oates snapped, and lured a 10-year-old boy named Lewis Hill into Leakin Park, there he raped him before slitting his throat. Still fighting the rage inside, he cut off the boy's head and hands, then engaged in necrophilia with the body parts.

The next day, he lured three more young boys into the park, eight-year-old Larry Jefferson, his five-year-old brother Mack, and 10-year-old Lester Watson. He took them to a secluded location, stabbed them to death, gutted them, and sliced off their genitals – which he took with him, but not before raping their corpses.

The very next day, despite police swarming the park, Oates lured two young girls to another secluded area. As he was attacking them, police were made aware of his location and caught him before he could kill the girls. Oates was arrested carrying two bags and a lunchbox, containing body parts of the murdered boys.

He was later convicted of four murders and multiple other connected crimes, and sentenced to confinement within a psychiatric hospital, where it is said he remains to this day. Now in his Seventies, no photo of him exists past 1968.

Other killings

In March 1979, the body of 23-year-old mother of one, Gwendolyn Moore, was found in a wooded area in the park, with multiple stab wounds. She had travelled from New York to visit friends and family. Despite a large investigation, her case remains unsolved.

In 1992, seven-year-old Timothy Washington was abducted from Leakin Park and murdered. For 14 years, it remained a cold case until Keith Garrett was arrested. He had taken Timothy to an empty shed in the park and killed him before burying him nearby. Despite a search, no body parts have ever been found.

In March 1993, the body of 31-year-old Linda Pearson was found on the side of the park, she had been strangled and beaten by her husband. Donn Pearson was arrested shortly after and sentenced to life in prison.

In April 2005, after an argument with his mother, 18-year-old Ross Telp stabbed her multiple times in their own home. He then wrapped her body in the fabric of a children's paddling pool, drove to Leakin Park, and dumped her in a ravine. He was caught after boasting to his friends.

For a mostly detailed list of the bodies and victims of Leakin Park, I'd highly recommend visiting Cham Green's Blog (link in bibliography), a local crime mapper and researcher who has a website dedicated to the Leakin Park bodies.

Unidentified serial killer

In May 1982, the body of 26-year-old Joyce Ann DeShields was found on a street beside Leakin Park, she had been strangled to death and left partially nude, to be discovered by young children playing in the area.

Over the following months, Baltimore police began linking similar murders across the city and came to the terrifying conclusion there was a serial killer at large in the area. Between 1981 and 1982, five murder victims were tentatively linked to the same killer.

The victims had all been strangled to death and their bodies left nude or partially nude. Despite the connection between them, the Baltimore Police – constantly overrun with murder cases – decided it was speculation only and never investigated the serial killer link. All cases remain unsolved.

There is a theory that exists of an unidentified serial killer active during the 1970s and 1980s across the United States, who would use notorious murder grounds to dump his victims. He did this to add to the body count of the areas, throw investigators off the scent, and add confusion to the mix.

There have been many murders in various so-called dumping grounds, including Leakin Park and the Texas Killing Fields, which remain unsolved to this day, and some are similar due to the method of murder and the time period when they were found.

It could be possible that a serial killer, maybe cleverer than others, has been using these locations to *hide* his victims, and as such, has never been caught.

Legacy of Leakin

From 2011, Baltimore officials began closing off areas of the park they deemed risky and introduced funding to regenerate the worst areas to make it better for visitors.

Something as simple as CCTV was never considered, and since 2011 at least seven more bodies have been found, two of them unsolved.

Since the 1940s, at least 10 murders still remain unsolved. The true number of bodies found in and around the park could number in the hundreds, which is horrifically plausible, as since 1977 alone, almost 10,000 people have been murdered in Baltimore.

Despite Leakin park welcoming new visitors and families on a daily basis, there is a darkness running through its roots that remains to this day. Yet, behind each body in the park, is a story, a family, a process of grief.

Though we may look and gasp in shock at what has occurred and is still occurring in Leakin Park, there are many hundreds more who have been directly impacted by the loss of loved ones, and the very mention of Leakin Park strikes fear and anger into their hearts.

Beachy Head Murder

A young woman disappeared near Beachy Head, a known suicide spot, but nine years later, her body is discovered on top of the cliffs, with links to an infamous serial killer.

Beachy Head

Eastbourne, on the South Coast of England, is a Victorian coastal town popular with tourists for its beaches and history. Its long promenade offers a pier, Victorian hotels, shops, and a shingle beach with sandy stretches at low tide.

Immediately to the west of the town is Beachy Head, the highest chalk sea cliffs in Great Britain, and part of the South Downs National Park, which stretches 87 miles along the coast to the ancient city of Winchester.

Though beautiful and alluring, attracting artists and writers from all over the world, Beachy Head harbours a darkness. Since the 7th Century, it has been Britain's most common suicide spot, and the third most common suicide spot in the world, after San Francisco's Golden Gate Bridge, and Japan's Aokigahara Woods.

On Wednesday 15th May 1980, 22-year-old Eastbourne College student Jessie Earl, disappeared from her bedsit and failed to return home the next morning. The London born student was known to take long walks up to Beachy Head where she would read and write about nature.

So when she disappeared, and a police search turned up no trace of her, it was suggested she had become part of the saddening statistics that had haunted Beachy Head for centuries. Until her remains were discovered on the cliff top nine years later.

1980

On the night of the 15th, Jessie had phoned her mother from a phone box on the seafront and told her that she would be home to London for a visit on the Friday. But on Saturday the 18th, when Jessie had failed to show up, and concerned for her whereabouts, her mother, Valerie, caught the train down to Eastbourne.

She arrived at Jessie's bedsit in Upperton Gardens and found her purse and personal belongings on the bed. Dirty dishes in the sink suggested she left them to soak before returning to clean them later, but she never returned, and her friends claimed they hadn't seen her since the Wednesday.

Jessie was officially reported missing and the police used sniffer dogs to search the bedsit for clues. Missing person posters were put up around town, and the media were informed that Jessie had failed to return home.

Police used helicopters and thermal imaging to search the South Downs on Beachy Head, expecting the worst, but there were no signs of Jessie anywhere. After three weeks, the investigation ground to a halt and it was left to the family to continue appealing for new information.

Valerie found Jessie's diary in the bedsit and it contained no suggestion she was suffering from ill mental health or considering suicide.

For nine years, Valerie, and her husband, John, refused to believe the suicide version of events.

1989

On a fresh March day in 1989, a family were flying kites on top of Beachy Head when one of the kites fell into a dense section of shrub land. When the father went to retrieve the kite, he discovered the skeletal remains of a human body.

A forensic investigation confirmed they were the remains of Jessie Earl. They discovered she had died at the scene and was found naked. The only item of clothing was a bra tied around her wrists, and all personal items such as her ring and watch were missing.

The investigation was so detailed that police cordoned off an area of land where she had been found and excavated the soil to search for clues that would have been left nine years earlier. They found nothing in the soil, and a local team of metal detectors came up short too.

Despite being found naked and with a bra tied around her wrists, the coroner later recorded an open verdict, as he could find no evidence to conclusively prove how she had died.

John Earl confirmed the family's stance that she had been murdered. *'Jesse didn't get herself killed by accident, suicide, or anything else. She was naked, she had been tied up with her bra. She was murdered.'*

Operation Anagram

Eleven years passed, and in 2000, the police launched a murder enquiry into the death of Jessie Earl, brought about by the appeals made by her family. However, the lead investigator admitted they had destroyed vital evidence.

Because Jessie's death was never officially classified as a murder, the forensic evidence had been destroyed in 1997, in line with police procedures. This included the bra, and some of the soil that had been removed from around the body. Due to the lack of forensic evidence, the case went nowhere.

Then in 2006, a convicted rapist, who had spent 14 years in prison for the assault and rape of two teenage girls in Leigh Park, Havant, was arrested for the murder of Angelika Kluk in Glasgow. His name was Peter Tobin, and he would soon become known as one of Britain's worst serial killers.

After his conviction in the same year for the murder of Angelika, a nationwide police investigation was set up to look at Tobin's life and movements before his first prison sentence, and in the years between being released and the 2006 victim.

They called this investigation; Operation Anagram, and it used multiple police forces and databases to link Tobin to dozens of murders and disappearances of teenage girls and young women across the United Kingdom. One of them was Jessie Earl.

One case he was positively linked to was 18-year-old Louise Kay who disappeared from none other than Beachy Head in 1988. Tobin was known to have been working at an Eastbourne hotel at the time and may have lured Louise to his home in Brighton, a few miles along the coast to the east.

Louise's body has never been found but is suspected to have been buried by Tobin at one of his properties.

A likely theory

In 2007, while searching one of Tobin's old houses in Bathgate, Scotland, they unearthed the bodies of 15-year-old Vicky Hamilton and Dinah McNicol, who had both disappeared in 1991. Vicky was found with her wrists tied together with a bra.

The similarities to the discovery of Jessie's remains were overwhelming but not conclusive. Operation Anagram investigators pored over Jessie's cases and confirmed Tobin was living in the area at the time. But without the evidence destroyed by the police, and no confession from Tobin, they could not charge him with the murder.

Operation Anagram went quiet in 2011 with no more victims to look at, and no new information coming to light. Since his arrest in 2006, Tobin has been convicted of three murders at different trials, with a suggestion he may have killed up to 10. He was sentenced to life imprisonment.

Jessie's family believe that Tobin may have been responsible for her death. But Tobin presents a problem. Many unsolved murders and disappearances from the 1970s and 1980s, tend to be at some point linked to Tobin and another British serial killer, Robert Black.

As Tobin and Black were active during that time period, and moved about a lot, it seems easy to match them up with various unsolved cases. But the problem comes when too many victims are laid at their feet, as it may hinder investigations looking elsewhere at other suspects or circumstances that could hold more truth.

In 2018, it was confirmed by local police that there was no hard evidence implicating Tobin or any other suspect in the murder of Jessie Earl. Despite the murder enquiries into Jessie's death, the official death certificate remains an open verdict, something her family are fighting to change.

It is possible and likely that Jessie was killed by Peter Tobin. It's also possible she was murdered by another unidentified killer, someone who has never been suspected. For over forty years, her murder has remained unsolved.

The only witness is Beachy Head itself, which continues to harbour the secrets of the dead, among hundreds of thousands of the living who visit for its beauty.

The One-Legged Man

A criminal fitted with an unbreakable GPS ankle tracker became the prime suspect in a murder, even though the GPS data reported he had never left his home – or at least, not all of him.

Sentinel

Before becoming the prime suspect in a murder that confused Washington DC authorities, Quincy Green was a known career criminal, with 25 arrests and 11 convictions to his name. Despite his long record, there was nothing quite as serious as murder on his list.

Arrested in early 2016 for carrying a gun without a license, Green was subsequently placed on high-intensity supervision (HISP). A system designed for high-risk offenders who – like Green – had previously broken the law while on probation or were eligible for work release from prison.

For Green, he was ordered to wear a Sentinel GPS tracker at all times and remain under house arrest at his residence until the end of the sentence. The OM400 ankle tracker is a commonly used offender-monitoring system that enables police to keep a track of high-risk offenders.

The anklet is considered the most reliable in the industry with two way communication between police and offender and tracked every minute of every day using a powerful satellite and relay system.

It's also used for proximity alerts when people are near to encroaching their boundary lines, and to inform domestic violence victims when their attacker is near. It is the most unfailing tracking system of its kind and any tampering of the device would result in the police being notified.

So, when Green was witnessed near the scene of a murder just one mile from where he was under house arrest, the police were baffled, as the GPS data reported he had never left his home – or at least, not all of him.

Rock-solid alibi

On 19th May, in Southeast Washington, 44-year-old Dana Hamilton was shot dead outside of his apartment block. Witnesses claimed to have seen someone with a similar appearance to Green nearby at the time.

But Green had a rock-solid alibi as he was at home at the time. Realising the witnesses could have been wrong, they checked the GPS data from the tracker around Green's leg, and the data backed-up his story, by showing that Green was indeed at home at the time of the murder.

But when investigators checked the CCTV footage near the crime scene, their jaws dropped to the ground in surprise. They watched as the surveillance showed Green with two men near the apartment block, joking and drinking.

Green then followed Dana as he walked down the street, then pulled a gun out and shot him multiple times. Police responded to the scene, and Dana was taken to a local hospital, where he subsequently succumbed to his injuries and was declared dead a short while later.

Further footage showed Green heading back to the direction of his home. But how was any of this possible as the tracker had not been removed from Green's leg?

There had been no tampering of the device and no efforts to break it. Yet, data showed that he was at home at the time of the murder. In fact, the data showed the device had barely moved at all.

The answer was as simple as it was bizarre – Green had simply taken off his leg.

A blunder

Six days after the murder, and sure they had the right man, police raided the home of Green and discovered the answer they were looking for. In a cupboard, they found a box, and inside was a prosthetic leg with the GPS tracker attached.

Green had been out and around town almost every night since his house arrest, by simply removing his prosthetic leg, where the tracker had been attached, and putting on another of his prosthetic legs.

When Green had been released from custody to house arrest, a security employee had mistakenly put the tracker over his sock. Any GPS tracker should be fitted to bare skin, and not over clothing. Had the security employee done this then they would have realised Green had a fake leg.

'It is frustrating for us as police officers to have one of our defendants released, especially when talking about dangerous crime like guns–and then to know that the accountability for these defendants isn't always up to par.' – Chairman of the D.C. Police Union.

Frustrating it might have been for the police, but for the family of Dana, it was a mistake that led to the murder of their loved one. Dana's mother said, *'it was the worst thing that ever happened to me.'*

Human error

According to official reports, it was the first known instance of a mistake being made while putting a GPS tracker on a convict. That the officers couldn't tell the difference between a real leg and a fake one is something of a concern and has since been put down to human error.

The security employee who wrongly placed the tracker over Green's sock was almost charged as an accessory to murder but the case went no further. The tracker's parent company, Sentinel Communications, were investigated for gross negligence but they too received no penalty.

In 2016, shortly after the death of Dana, Green solicited the murder of a fiancée of a witness to the shooting. For that solicitation, he was sentenced to three years, which gave prosecutors enough time to build a case against him – knowing he wasn't going anywhere.

In 2019, without a leg to stand on, Green was convicted of Dana's murder and sentenced to 17 years in prison. After the prison term, Green will be placed five years of supervised release – and one hopes that if police use a GPS tracker, then they make sure to put it on his real leg.

First Case of Hacking in History

People gathered in anticipation for the first public demo of the wireless telegram system, only for the world's first hacker to tap the signal – and use Morse code to insult the inventor!

Telegrams

Long gone are the days of using telegrams to send messages across great distances, we're fortunate enough in the digital age to be able to send emails or even texts across the world in a matter of micro-seconds.

In the early 20th Century, things weren't that simple. Telegrams started out in the telegraph age when telecommunication consisted of short messages transmitted by hand over the telegraph wire. They were sent between telegraph services; companies that delivered messages to the recipients.

Charged by the amount of words in the message, telegrams consisted of abbreviations with no punctuation, and minimal words. The very first telegram to be sent was from Orville Wright, on 17th December 1903, about the first powered air flight.

'Success four flights thursday morning all against twenty one mile wind started from Level with engine power alone average speed through air thirty one miles longest 57 seconds inform Press home Christmas.'

Six months earlier, in June 1903, when the telegram system was being showcased in front of eminent individuals and the public in London, someone hacked the network – and insulted the Italian scientist Guglielmo Marconi, who was conducting the test.

Marconi's demonstration

We don't often think of hackers as top-hat wearing men born in the 19th Century but the similarities in the way security hackers are used hasn't really changed much since then. The systems and capabilities we have now are vastly different but they still need to be security tested.

Most hackers as we think of them nowadays, are mostly security experts, who look for flaws in company systems, or in the development of new software. And in 1903, things were not much different.

Though computers didn't exist, avenues of communication did, in the same way modern-day companies are protecting their digital footprint, so did olden-day companies wish to protect their communication lines.

Guglielmo Marconi was a Nobel Prize winning Italian scientist, born in 1874 Bologna, who is known as the inventor of radio. He pioneered long distance radio transmission and developed the very first wireless telegraph system using electromagnetic waves – as dot/dashes of the Morse code.

On that summers day in 1903, some of the world's leading scientists and members of the public were gathered in the lecture hall of the Royal Institution in London, ready to showcase the new Telegram system to the world. Marconi was waiting 300 miles away on a hill in Cornwall, ready to send a message to the eager onlookers.

The system had undergone immense testing, and back in 1901, Marconi had sent the first wireless signals across the Atlantic. Now it was time to show the public it worked, to dispel rumours that the wireless telegraph was unsafe. But someone else had other ideas.

Diddling the public

Moments before the demonstration was about to begin, the equipment kicked into life and began tapping out a message, which shocked the onlookers – and the scientists. At first, the word RATS was repeated over and over again. Then, the telegram got personal.

As the scientists gawped in confusion, a message came over the system that said; *'there was a young fellow of Italy, who diddled the public quite prettily.'* Then it is claimed the message continued to rant but no record of it exists beyond the line above.

Being 300 miles away, Marconi was unaware of the intrusion, and continued with the demonstration, but the damage had already been done. When Marconi found out, he was furious.

His very public demonstration had been hacked – or tapped, as was the slang of the day, and the hacker had personally attacked him. Marconi had promised confidential communication channels sent on a frequency that could not have been intercepted.

Someone had tapped into the Royal Institution using strong enough wireless signals to interfere with the equipment's electric arc discharge lamp. But who could have pulled off such an extraordinary feat?

Enter British magician and inventor, Nevil Maskelyne.

Scientific vandalism

Born in 1863, Nevil was a descendant of a long line of British illusionists and inventors. He had been following Marconi's work and wireless technology for some time, purely for the purposes of incorporating it into his magic shows.

He would use Morse code during his shows to communicate with his assistant and team behind the stage, to pull off tricks that wowed his audience. In a book about his mostly unrecorded life, there is a story that he was able to send a radio message from the ground to a hot-air balloon, using equipment he had invented himself.

While Nevil was developing his own wireless system, Marconi managed to get broad patents for the technology, which meant Nevil couldn't develop his systems further. Yet, it wasn't Nevil's idea to hack the demonstration, it was at the request of the British-owned Eastern Telegraph Company.

They were worried the Marconi system wasn't as confidential as it was claimed to be and were aggrieved at having spent a fortune laying cables meant for the previous wired telegraphic system. Hearing of Nevil's work, they commissioned him to prove that Marconi's technology had flaws.

Nevil invented a 25-metre radio antenna that he used to intercept Marconi's test signals. On the day of the demonstration, he used the antenna and signal to taunt Marconi at his demonstration.

Gentleman hacker

An investigation followed where Marconi publicly requested people to unmask the criminal who had gone against all codes of science to ruin his life's work – and mock him! It didn't take long because Nevil was proud of what he had done and admitted to it.

He wrote a letter to a newspaper claiming his intention was to unmask Marconi and reveal the flaws within the so-called private communication system. He ended the letter saying it was for the common good of all mankind.

For many months and years that followed, Marconi persisted that Nevil was an insult to science and should have been arrested for his crimes. However, as with many hackers today, he was commissioned to find flaws in a new technology – which he did.

Marconi went on to win the 1909 Nobel Prize in Physics with Karl Ferdinand Braun for their contributions to the development of wireless telegraphy. In 1931, he set up Vatican Radio for Pope Pius XI, six years before his death in 1937.

Nevil went on to continue his illustrious career in magic, wrote several books on the subject, and died peacefully in 1924. The two men's paths were forever entwined, and due to their rivalry, it is perhaps no surprise that the first hacking in history was used to send an insult.

Soul Eater and the Runaway Devil

A man claiming to be a 300-year-old vampire, and a 12-year-old girl, fell into a forbidden love which left the girl's entire family murdered – a dark tale that concludes with a disturbing twist.

Besotted with death

There is nothing more disturbing than a child who commits pre-meditated murder, except perhaps a child who commits murder with an adult boyfriend who believed he was a vampire.

In Medicine Hat, Alberta, Canada, on 23rd April 2006, 12-year-old Jasmine Richardson and her 23-year-old boyfriend Jeremy Steinke killed three members of Jasmine's family. They had spent many weeks planning the murders in revenge for Jasmine's parents disapproving of their relationship.

Jasmine looked older for her age and was known to go out with friends to rock concerts, and it was there she allegedly met the 23-year-old Jeremy, just three months before the murders. Jasmine set up user profiles on the Vampire Freaks forum, and a Canadian forum and messaging board called Nexopia.

On both sites she listed her age as 15 and used it as a way to converse with Jeremy, and their relationship grew to the point where Jasmine became besotted with the idea of murder, propagated by a love of blood and a fascination with human anatomy. She went under the username of Runaway Devil, while Jeremy used Soul Eater, among others.

Jeremy too had some unusual preferences. He was known to enjoy the taste of blood and carried around a small vial of his own blood around his neck for whenever the hunger struck. He told his friends that he was a 300-year-old vampire, lost in time, just trying to survive in the new world.

Natural Born Killers

When Jasmine's parents found out about the burgeoning relationship, they tried to stop Jasmine seeing Jeremy, but it didn't end well. That fascination with blood, led Jasmine to believe her parents needed to die as punishment for telling her what to do and trying to end her relationship.

Jeremy was fascinated with the Oliver Stone movie Natural Born Killers, about a young couple who kill the lead female's parents then go on a killing spree. He believed that he and his new young girlfriend should use the film as a starting point for their life together.

They planned the murder of Jasmine's family and thought of it as the right thing to do, to rid themselves of imposing mortals who would do nothing to stop their forbidden love.

In some of her messages to Jeremy, Jasmine shared photographs of herself holding a gun and posing in gothic makeup. The love between them was seemingly growing stronger in her heart. Just hours before the murders, she posted; 'welcome to my tragic end'.

The same morning, at his trailer, Jeremy watched Natural Born Killers again. He told his friends that he and Jasmine should go about their plans for murder in the same way. He also claimed the film to be the greatest love story of all time.

Bloodstained house

On the morning of the 23rd, Jeremy and Jasmine met up, went to her parents' house and stabbed to death her father, 42-year-old Marc Richardson, her mother, 48-year-old Debra, and Jasmine's brother, eight-year-old Tyler.

Police arrived shortly after when a friend of the family discovered the bodies inside the bloodstained house. The parents were found in the basement, stabbed to death, and Tyler was found on the first floor of the property with his throat cut.

Jasmine was thought to be missing, and as such she was suspected to have been kidnapped and killed elsewhere. When police began searching for her, they came across the messages between her and Jeremy, and shockingly realised she had been involved in the murders.

The following day, the pair were arrested in Leader, Saskatchewan, approximately 80 miles south of the Richardson house. Steinke had enlisted the help of friend and drug addict, 19-year-old Kacy Lancaster, to drive them away in her pick-up truck – along with three underage friends.

Lancaster was later charged as being an accessory to murder but the charges were dropped for the focus to remain on Jeremy and Jasmine. Shortly after the arrests, Jeremy asked Jasmine to marry him, and still besotted with her 300-year-old vampire, she agreed.

Punishments

While claiming to be innocent, Jeremy fell into the trap of confessing to an undercover police officer placed in his cell, where he told the officer he had killed the parents. He was ultimately found guilty on three counts of first-degree murder in 2008, and sentenced to three life sentences, one for each of the victims.

Jasmine's trial was a little trickier. At the time, her name could not be published due to limitations in the Youth Criminal Justice Act. In Canada, any person under the age of 14 at the time of a crime cannot be sentenced as an adult.

In July 2007, a whole year before Jeremy was convicted, the then 13-year-old Jasmine was found guilty of three counts of first-degree murder, the youngest person in Canada to be convicted of multiple first-degree murders. She was sentenced to the maximum allowable term of ten years in a psychiatric institution.

In the Autumn of 2011, Jasmine was released from the institution and spent the next four-and-a half-years under a community rehabilitation order. On 6th May 2016, aged 22, Jasmine was released of any further court orders and conditions, and freed to live her life.

But let's step back for a moment, because there is more to this case than meets the eye and you were promised a twist in the blurb. It doesn't matter how readers or researchers look at the case, it is horrific and disturbing. Yet, the deeper we dig into the Richardson case, the more disturbing it could actually be.

As crazy as he was

Newspaper reports at the time and court documents reveal that something else may have been going on with the pair. It's easy to forget that a 12-year-old girl – a child – was involved in these killings, however we have to look at where we draw the line of innocence. It's also important to remember that Jasmine was found guilty of committing three pre-meditated murders.

As they fled Medicine Hat, one of the underage children in the pick-up truck, testified that a newspaper report of the murders brought smiles to the faces of the killers, and they jested over the fact the paper had used Jasmine's old school photograph.

On the morning of the murders, when Jeremy was watching Natural Born Killers, his friends testified about a phone call they overheard. They claimed he was on the phone in the kitchen pacing back and forth, panicking about something they couldn't understand at the time.

He was heard saying, '*I don't want to do this. Are you sure you want to do this*?' The same witness claimed that Jasmine was the one who begged Jeremy to do it – for her.

Returning to watch the film, he sat down during a scene where the lead female, played by Juliette Lewis, spares her younger brother. Jeremy pointed at the screen and said, '*that's where we would do it different. She (Jasmine) would kill her brother.*'

Many of the friends claimed he spoke about killing Jasmine's parents as she wouldn't be strong enough to kill the adults, but she could kill her brother. The friends tried to talk him out of it but were unsure if he would go through with any of it, or if he was even being genuine.

He told his friends they wouldn't understand, and in Jasmine, he had found someone as crazy as he was. In some ways, he was right.

Manipulative sociopath

Jasmine was convicted of first-degree murder a year before Jeremy based on the testimony of some of the people who later testified at Jeremy's trial. Even after the story had come out, it was insinuated by the press that Jeremy alone had killed all three victims.

According to Jeremy and some of the witnesses, it was Jasmine who had masterminded the plan for the murders. Jasmine was known to be manipulative, cold, and sociopathic, but couldn't be described as such because her brain was considered to still be developing.

In fact, at Jasmine's trial, she admitted to killing her younger brother while he begged for his life. Tyler pleaded with her that he was '*too young to die*' but Jasmine slit his throat and watched his blood splatter the bedsheets.

Jeremy claimed that when she slit her brother's throat, '*it didn't bother her at all, she didn't cry or anything. In fact, the next day when we were on the road, she was laughing about it. She's got a few screws loose, too.*'

Could a 12-year-old girl have been so numbed by death that she manipulated a 23-year-old man into killing her family? It's possible but both of them had long been on a dark road.

Descent

Jeremy lived on a trailer park with his mother, and she said Jeremy was abused and beaten by her husband, his father, when he was younger. He had been on anti-depressants for over a decade, was a high-school dropout, and was known to be younger than his age with a sense of gullibility about him.

Even so, he stabbed Debra Richardson 12 times and left her at the bottom of the basement staircase before stabbing Marc 24 times. Their blood covered the walls as he followed his girlfriend up the stairs to her brother's room.

Even in the few months he had been with Jasmine, he dreamed of marrying her in a Gothic wedding ceremony and moving to a castle in Germany, where they could live out their dark fantasies in any way they pleased.

Growing up, Jasmine was a happy, intelligent girl until the age of 11, when she descended into an obsession with violence, became sexually active, and found solace in the world of the mythical vampire, besotted with blood.

On her profile pages of the forums, her interests were blood, darkness, human anatomy, serial killers, hatchets, criminal psychology, and '*kinky shit*'. Her heroes were Jeffrey Dahmer, Marilyn Manson, and Dani Filth from UK-based metal group, Cradle of Filth; her favourite band.

She refused to wear school uniforms and instead went around wearing short skirts, heavy black makeup, and told people she was 15 or 16, depending on what she thought she could get away with.

Lust for blood

Vampiric tendency is something occasionally noted in psychology under some cases of schizophrenia and linked to Renfield Syndrome. A patient generally displays a strong desire for blood and believes they are consuming the lifeforce of others or replenishing their own.

It is questionable why Jeremy's lawyer didn't base his defence on insanity, as Jeremy clearly had mental issues in the past, evident from the medication. He was also clearly displaying some signs of a psychological disorder, evident by his blood consumption.

Many find it disturbing that a 12-year-old girl would become so consumed by her own lust for blood, that she used a 23-year-old man to kill her parents because she wasn't strong enough, and even more worrying that she is now free to walk among us unsupervised.

Jasmine had grown up too fast, consumed by the darkness she surrounded herself with, believing it to be the best life for her. Unable to decipher art from reality, she fell into a dark web of blood lust and forbidden love.

Jeremy had long been seeking the missing half of his own dark soul, and when he found Jasmine, regardless of her age, he connected on a level beyond lust and passion, and found the person he was happy to call crazier than he was.

Together, they carved a path through the annals of true crime history that has since been unmatched in its depravity and shamefulness, underpinned by a somewhat depressing tale of two lovers under the darkness of the full moon.

'My biggest fear is that she hasn't been rehabilitated, that she's tricked those in the system, that she hasn't moved forward.' – Brent Secondiak, the first police officer to arrive at the Richardson home.

Battle of Lanarca Airport

Forced to return with the plane they had hijacked, two assassins and their hostages watched from the windows in shock, as special forces opened fire – on each other.

Assassins turned hijackers

One day before the hijacking, on 18th February 1978, Egyptian writer and former Minister of Culture, Yusuf Sibai, attended an Asian-African conference in Nicosia, Cyprus. Without warning, two assassins breached the perimeter and shot him dead.

They then rounded up thirty members of the delegation, in attendance at the Solidarity Conference, and held them hostage in the Hilton Hotel restaurant. They demanded that Cypriot authorities fly them out of the country or they would start killing the hostages with grenades.

Among the hostages were two members of the Palestine Liberation Organisation (PLO), and at least one Egyptian national. The assassins demanded a Cyprus Airways Douglas DC8 aircraft, and in the early hours of the 19th, the Cypriot authorities gave in to their demands.

The assassins and their hostages were transported to Larnaca International Airport where the plane was waiting. The hostages were under threat of death by grenade and at no point along the journey was there a window of opportunity to end the siege.

After further negotiations, the assassins boarded the plane with 11 hostages and four crew members, including two pilots. Cyprus authorities watched with anger and frustration, as the plane took off.

But just a few hours later, the plane returned.

Denied

The assassins had been seeking refuge in Syria and ordered the pilot to land in the city of Djibouti. Air traffic controllers and the Syrian authorities denied permission for the plane to land. It was forced to fly over the city and turn back for plan B.

Plan B was Saudi Arabia, though not the assassins first choice, it was a country where they would not be extradited. But Saudi officials had been informed by Egyptian officials not to let the plane land. After a heated exchange, Saudi Arabia also denied permission for the plane to land, and ordered it be shot out of the sky should it attempt to.

Sheepishly – and due to low fuel – the pilots informed the assassins they had to return to Cyprus as nowhere else would take them. Just a few hours after they had left, the aircraft returned to Larnaca Airport, where it waited in stillness on the runway.

Behind the scenes, things were not so still. The Cypriot army had been called in and were beginning efforts to surround the plane and end the siege peacefully. Politically, things were about to get confusing – as they always would.

Force-17 & Task Force 777

After hearing that two PLO members were among the hostages, PLO leader Yasser Arafat, who would later become the first President of the Palestinian National Authority, made a personal phone call to the Cypriot President Spyros Kyprianou.

Arafat offered the services of a hit squad of twelve Force-17 gunmen; a commando and special operations unit. Kyprianou, already losing control of the situation, agreed to Arafat's terms, and ordered a passenger airliner be sent to Beirut to collect them.

The Force-17 squad arrived in secret at Larnaca Airport just a few hours later. The squad were kept out of sight in a terminal building, on the off-chance that the Cypriot army could not negotiate the assassins' surrender.

Moments after Arafat had phoned Kyprianou, the Egyptian President, Anwar Sadat, also had something to say. The victim in the assassination, Yusuf Sibai, was a close friend of Sadat, and he wasn't best pleased with the way Cyprus had handled the situation thus far.

He begged Kyprianou to resolve the hijacking, rescue the hostages, and extradite the assassins to Egypt. Kyprianou confirmed he would do everything he could, and even travelled to the airport himself to oversee operations.

Yet, unbeknownst to Kyprianou, Sadat had ordered a C-130 Hercules military aircraft to depart Cairo with an Egyptian elite commando squad named Task Force 777. Egyptian officials told Cyprus that some people were on the way to help rescue the hostages – and that was all they said.

Disaster

With elite squads from three separate countries sharing the same tarmac, tensions were already rising. However, unknown to the Egyptians, at the time Task Force 777 landed at the airport, the Cypriot authorities had already negotiated the surrender of the hijackers.

Just moments before the surrender was finalised and the hostages would have been rescued, Task Force

777 launched an all-out assault on the aircraft. A military jeep burst out of the Hercules military plane, followed by an estimated 60 elite Egyptian Commandos on foot.

The Cypriot army caught sight of the Egyptians charging towards the hijacked plane and were given orders to respond, as the Egyptian military had not been given clearance to engage on Cypriot soil. They issued two loud verbal warnings to the Egyptians, who ignored them and moved closer to the plane.

On board the craft, the two hijackers and hostages, were preparing to leave the plane, as the surrender had been negotiated. Suddenly, as they peered through the small windows, all hell broke loose outside.

The streak of an RPG missile lit up the runway and hit the Egyptian jeep, sending it up into the air with the force of the explosion. Gunfire then erupted across the airport, as both Cypriot and Egyptian forces began attacking each other.

The Battle of Larnaca

The Egyptian Task Force 777 were already at a disadvantage. The jeep had been blown to smithereens, and they were left exposed on the tarmac. The prime-positioned Cypriot army rained down a hail of bullets and grenades on to the Egyptians.

Vexed at the situation, the Cypriots ordered a tank to take out the Egyptian plane. They opened fire on the Hercules, before the tank hit the nose of the aircraft with an anti-tank missile, exploding the front of the plane and rendering it destroyed.

With their aircraft destroyed, the Egyptian force and the Cypriot special forces continued fighting for at least another hour, with the remainder of the Egyptians taking cover in empty planes nearby. Kyprianou, who was in the control tower, watched the events unfold with horror. The tower was also shot at by the Egyptians, which could have resulted in an even worse event.

The Egyptians themselves were forced to surrender due to the minimal equipment they had brought with them. Their orders had been to bring the hijackers back to Cairo and rescue the hostages, not involve themselves in a potential war.

As the dust settled, 20 Egyptian special commandos had been killed, including three in the jeep and three in the Hercules. 15 more were wounded, and one Hercules aircraft was destroyed along with the military jeep. There were no casualties on the Cypriot side, apart from a few injuries.

Severed

The day after, on 20th February, relations between Egypt and Cyprus were severed. Egypt immediately cut ties with Cyprus, and ended its diplomatic mission in the country, with Cyprus doing the same to Egypt shortly after.

Kyprianou later offered apologies to Egypt but insisted that he could not allow a foreign military to act without permission on Cypriot soil. Syria, who blocked the flight from landing, along with Libya, condemned Egypt's actions.

For three years, the ties remained severed until Anwar's unconnected assassination in 1981. The two countries have since developed better political relationships. After the attack, it was suggested that the PLO special forces, who were hiding in the terminal, may also have helped the Cypriot army to fight the Egyptians.

Though it was never proven true, the consequences of Palestine being involved in a fight against Egypt would have been even more severe. Yet, the Cypriots claimed they had not fired a single shot.

As for the assassins turned hijackers, they were arrested on the plane by the Cypriots, and led off through the warzone of Lanarca Airport. After all the fighting, miscommunication, and deaths, the two men were later extradited to Egypt anyway, where they ultimately received a life sentence.

Nude in the Nettles

A strange phone call leads to the discovery of a woman's body on the North York Moors, but for over 40 years, her identity and death remain a mystery, and one of England's oddest unsolved cold cases.

National security

North Yorkshire, in England, is home to the North York Moors National Park, with rolling green landscapes and windy fields. Nestled in the Hambleton District of the North York Moors is Sutton Bank, a hill with extensive views over the Vale of York and the Vale of Mowbray.

Close by is Roulston Scar, an Iron Age hill fort built in the 5th Century, a place of historical interest where the Battle of Old Byland took place, in which the Scots mounted an attack and defeated the forces of King Edward II.

Fifteen Centuries later, on the morning of 28th August 1981, Constable John Jeffries of Ripon Police had arrived at the station to start his shift. Shortly after, he received a phone call from a well-spoken man with a trace of a local Yorkshire accent.

He said, '*near Scawton Moor House, you will find a decomposed body among the willow herbs.*' Unsure what to make of it, Jeffries asked for the man's name and address. To which the reply was, '*I cannot divulge this information for reasons of national security*', before hanging up.

Before the man had hung up, he had provided detailed instructions on where they could find the body. When Jeffries took it to his superiors, they suggested the onus was on him to find it. He walked up to Sutton Bank, and there among the willow herbs, he found human bones.

Remains

The search hadn't been easy, Jeffries had scoured the area for an hour before discovering the remains, packed tightly into the sprawling bushes around the area. Detective Chief Superintendent Strickland Carter was called to the scene with his CID squad, who mounted a large operation.

They spent almost half a day removing the willow herbs and shrubbery from around the bones and used a team to scour Sutton Bank in search for further remains. Then, near to the top of the hill, close to Scawton Moor House, beside a country road, they found a decomposed body.

With the Yorkshire Ripper, Peter Sutcliffe, having been arrested seven months earlier, murder was fresh on Carter's mind. Though Sutcliffe had been active in Yorkshire, he was not known to have ventured to the area around Sutton Bank.

An investigation discovered the body was that of a female and that she would have been nude at the time of her death, suggesting foul play. But there seemed to be no knife marks on the bones nor had her skull been crushed by a blunt object. There were no clothes nearby, she had no jewellery, and no identifying piece of evidence.

Due to the decomposition of the body, and the rate the willow herbs had grown up around it, it was suggested she had died at least one year earlier. This was confirmed when they removed the body and found a yogurt pot underneath her, with a sell-by-date of 1979.

Sutton Bank Body

Even though Sutton Bank was popular with hikers and families on picnics, the body had remained undisturbed for nearly two years. Due to the Ripper case being fresh in the memories of the detectives, they made sure to thoroughly detail the crime scene, with hundreds of photos.

As soon as the media got hold of the story, the mystery of the Nude in the Nettles was born. Despite nettles and willow herbs being two very different species of plants, an eager reporter may have been close to the police boundary, saw some nettles nearby and came up with the name.

It's remarkable how many names and monikers of serial killers, cold cases, unidentified bodies, and other crimes, are given to us by newspapers and the media – mostly to sell more copies or get more views on a website.

Some more conservative newspapers ran with *Sutton Bank Body*, though it was the Nude in the Nettles that drew more people in. Due to the fact she was nude, police suspected she had been murdered but had no evidence to go on, or motive.

More importantly, the identity of the woman was a mystery. The only link they had to the body was the mystery phone caller who led them there. But before the days of phone tracking, whether the man was simply a good Samaritan or someone involved in the murder, we'll never know.

Reconstruction

Due to the media attention, the profile of the case was lifted and the public became invested. This gave local police the impetus to hold press conferences in which they appealed to the public if they knew of any woman who had disappeared in the past two years.

Unsurprisingly they were overrun with phone calls and messages to the local station with no solid leads materialising. Detective Carter had recently read an Egyptian article where scientists had reconstructed the face of an ancient Mummy, and thought it was a good idea.

Though facial reconstruction had been around since 1883, it was mostly used in archaeology. It wasn't until 1962 that scientist Wilton Krogman popularised it in the field of forensics. The subsequent facial reconstruction of the Nude in the Nettles was a landmark moment in UK forensics.

But it didn't help the case, even after releasing the image to the public. During the investigation, some items of clothing, including underwear, were found hanging on a tree less than a mile away, but again – there was no evidence to suggest the clothing belonged to the woman.

One possible identity for the victim was an escaped prisoner named Geraldine Crawley, who escaped from Askham Grange prison in 1979. But when they made the name public, Geraldine herself sent a letter to the police with her fingerprints claiming she was alive – eventually leading to her recapture.

4601

In 2012, after advances in forensic testing and DNA technology had reached a good enough level, the body of the unidentified woman was exhumed. She had been buried in a council cemetery, under a small headstone displaying '4601', the identifier of her position among the dead.

A full DNA profile was able to be extracted which gave investigators the opportunity to compare the results with potential families, and to add the profile to the national DNA database. Despite comparing it to people who claimed the woman was a family member, there were no matches.

With the advances of genealogy websites and larger DNA databases, the police are still hopeful that one day, the woman and the cause of her death may be identified.

The police have since confirmed that there were no missing person reports that matched the description of the woman at the time she had died. It remains a mystery why no one would have reported her missing unless something darker was afoot.

Unsolved

The location the body was found was close to a by-road heading to the popular tourist town of Scarborough, a place visited by people from all over the country. It was deemed a possibility, that the woman was killed elsewhere, taken by car along a country road near to a tourist town, and left in a patch of willow herb close to the road.

And what about Peter Sutcliffe? On 4th April 1979, Sutcliffe killed 19-year-old Josephine Whitaker on Savile Park Moor in Halifax, 70 miles away from Sutton Bank.

Later that year, on 1st September, he murdered 20-year-old Barbara Leach and dumped her body under a pile of bricks in Bradford. He killed some of his victims with a screwdriver by stabbing them in the neck and abdomen, parts of the body that wouldn't leave marks on the bones.

He murdered at least 13 women between the ages of 16 and 47, an age bracket the Nude in the Nettles fell into. He mostly killed prostitutes, which may have explained why no one had reported the woman missing, as she may have been estranged from her family.

However, Sutcliffe never spoke of the unidentified body on Sutton Bank and was never questioned about it. Police at the time were just happy to have caught him and taken him off the streets. Perhaps their insistence the mystery caller was the killer took them away from the Sutcliffe possibility.

A frustrating aspect of the case materialised in the days after the body was found. In 1979, a local horse-rider had passed the patch where the body was later found and noticed a terrible smell. He was going to return later that day to investigate but fell off his horse and broke his leg.

He forgot about the incident until he watched the news two years later. Had he found the body at the time, then there would have been a strong possibility the case would have been solved. As it is, the Nude in the Nettles remains Yorkshire's most mysterious unsolved cold case.

Cult of the Black Lords

A female cult leader who taught 'Conscious Development' to fight the Black Lords, was accused of mind control murder, after many of her followers died, and left her everything they owned.

Conscious Development

Cults come in all shapes and sizes, some take the headlines and have thousands of followers, others are made up of groups of similar-thinking people across the world. Some, like the Cult of the Black Lords, are rarely spoken about, and yet, the cult left victims in its wake.

Though never really having a name, the devotees to Terri Lee Hoffman's cult, were taught a new religious movement called Conscious Development of Body, Mind and Soul, leading some researchers to call the cult 'Conscious Development'.

Terri's aim in the teachings was to train her devotees to be ready to fight against the black lords that she said existed on various different astral planes of existence and reality. She claimed to protect her followers with powerful gems and led them to believe she could save them.

The black lords were constantly trying to get at her and her followers, and it was up to them to try and halt the impending doom. Terri claimed the goal of the training was to die, to leave the physical body, battle the black lords, and join God and the Twelve Masters through reincarnation on a spiritual level.

Count me in – said at least one hundred people who attended her talks in Dallas, Texas. And this was before expanding to other American States. But when many of her followers died under mysterious circumstances, the authorities came knocking, and murder by mind control was suspected.

Dallas

Terri was born in 1938 and grew up in an orphanage as her parents were in severe poverty at the time. When she was only 16, she married truck driver John Wilder and they had three children together. By 1971, aged 33, she was committed to a psychiatric hospital relating to issues from her divorce to Wilder.

Though her personal life was full of trauma and issues, it was her passion that got her through life. From her late teens, and through her Twenties, she became besotted with hypnotism, mind control, and meditation.

In the late 1960s, she began writing and talking about her research into meditation and the mind. And by 1974, three years after being discharged from the hospital, she turned mind control into a business. She formed *Conscious Development of Body, Mind and Soul* as an official not-for-profit organisation.

Under the banner of Conscious Development, she began private consultations with individuals and taking payment for group lessons. At the same time, she opened a jewellery business to account for what she was to do next.

Realising her students were latching onto her every word, and willing to pay good money for her teachings, she ordered them to bring her expensive jewellery that she would then turn into powerful gemstones – said to heal and aid them as they developed further.

Teacher to cult leader

From 1975, an estimated 120 people regularly attended her weekly lectures in Dallas, and she spread the word of her classes by handing out printed information to the public. As her following grew, so did her ambition and she began to market herself as the reincarnation of Saint Teresa of Jesus, a Spanish Saint from the 16th Century.

She told her following they were all fighting a spiritual battle against the black lords, helped by God and the Twelve Masters, though there is no record as to who or what the Twelve Masters, or indeed the black lords were.

Playing into her cult aspirations, she claimed she could communicate with the dead, and see time as a construct where the past and future melded into one. But the main aspect of her teachings was that death was not to be feared because the sole purpose in life was to be reborn in the spiritual realm, and one could only do that by dying.

Yet, she needed proof that the black lords were contaminating her followers souls. She needed a reason to keep them coming back, a reason for them to keep providing her with expensive items and money, she needed a victim.

Death cult

In 1976, Terri and one of her inner circle followers visited Terri's second estranged husband, Glenn Cooley, at his cabin. The next day, Cooley was found dead of an apparent Valium and Librium overdose, supposedly administered by himself.

She then convinced many of her followers that the black lords were pushing closer to the earthly realm, evidenced by the fact that Cooley's blood had been poisoned. She claimed he was tainted because he was thinking negative thoughts, which allowed the black lords closer.

A week after the death, it was revealed that Cooley – though separated from Terri – had left his entire estate and financial assets to her in his will, which was in Terri's secure safe. She then convinced many of her followers that regular blood-letting was needed to allow the black lords poison to exit their systems.

Terri married her third husband five months later, a relationship that lasted for just over three years. In 1979, one of her inner circle followers, Sandra Cleaver, went on holiday with her daughter, Susan. Susan was not involved in the cult, as Sandra was worried about Susan's evil spirits infecting Terri.

While rafting on a lake, Susan mysteriously drowned after supposedly falling from the raft. Sandra then revealed that the sole beneficiary of Susan's $125,000 trust, was Terri and her group.

The will was deemed illegal by the authorities as Susan was too young to have signed it, leading to suspicions that Sandra had killed her daughter so the cult could benefit from the money.

Sandra then took out a $300,000 life insurance policy naming Terri as the sole beneficiary, along with the ownership of her own home. Then, a couple of weeks later in 1981, Sandra drove her car off the edge of a cliff, killing herself and her housekeeper.

The Black Lords

When Sandra's family contested the will, police investigated and claimed the document was created as a result of illegal influence by Terri, though it couldn't be proved. She was taken to court to contest the will but in the end the case was settled in her favour.

Three followers who testified for Terri at the trial were later found to have killed themselves under suspicious circumstances. They each left a substantial amount of money and assets to Terri and the group.

By 1982, the Conscious Development group had expanded into Chicago, and hundreds more people became involved in the spiritual teachings of Terri, along with the fear of the black lords that she put into people.

In 1987, the deaths increased. A follower named Robin Ostott was convinced by Terri that her best friend's invisible CIA lover was in league with the black lords and was working against her to end her life. Two days after visiting Terri, who convinced her that death was the pathway for reincarnation, Ostott shot herself in the head – and named Terri as the beneficiary of her will.

Later in 1987, a Chicago follower named Mary Levinson died from a suspicious overdose. When police investigated, they discovered her life insurance policy had been changed to her new boyfriend, who was becoming close to Terri.

In September 1988, Terri's fourth husband, Don Hoffman, was found dead from a drug overdose. In his letters, it was discovered that Terri told him that the black lords had infected him with cancerous cells and he was terminal. An autopsy discovered no traces of cancer. When questioned, Terri didn't deny anything, and said the black lords had hidden the cancer through illusion at the autopsy.

And guess what? Terri was the sole beneficiary of her fourth husband's estate. But four days later, former follower Jill Bounds was found beaten to death, with some pages ripped out of her diary that the killer had removed. Most pages were relating to the Cult of the Black Lords.

In June 1989, a couple named David and Glenda Goodman, who had been followers of Terri's for many years, took their own lives, having previously claimed their souls were ready for reincarnation in the spiritual realm.

Mind control

The children of Don Hoffman opened a wrongful death lawsuit against Terri in 1990, and a four-year criminal investigation by the Dallas District Attorney's Office got underway. Though they could link Terri and the group to multiple deaths that were clearly suspicious, they had no real evidence of wrongdoing.

It was clear to investigators that Terri had been manipulating many of her followers to take their own lives and will her their assets. Yet, many prosecutors, and an Assistant District Attorney claimed that it would be near-impossible to legally convict someone of having killed another through mind control.

Due to the rising costs of battling the lawsuit, Terri filed for bankruptcy in 1991, and in 1994 was sentenced to one year in prison for bankruptcy fraud, as it turned out there was more money in the Conscious Development accounts that she hadn't admitted to.

Terri married her fifth husband in 2002 and went on to spread the word of the Conscious Development through a website, before her death in 2015. The cult and website no longer exists.

The question remains whether Terri had used a form of mind control to convince her followers to take their own lives, lest the black lords get them. Or whether the group was simply beset by grim coincidences. But if true crime stories, and especially bizarre true crime stories, have taught us anything, it's that coincidence is a rare beast indeed.

With tales of missing diary pages, changes to life insurance and will beneficiaries, a murder among the group, and dead followers, it's a surprise the Cult of the Black Lords are not more well known, but perhaps now, for the victims, that can be changed.

Shoe Fetish Slayer

The dark tale of a killer, whose overpowering fetish for women's shoes, led him to abduct and murder his victims while dressed as a woman – before committing unspeakable acts against their corpses.

Women's shoes

Fetishes are common throughout the world, they can develop prior to adolescence but generally appear during puberty. Some psychologists believe that fetishism develops from early childhood experiences, normally with an object associated with sexual arousal or gratification.

These gratification objects are then connected with sexual maturity as a person ages. Fetishes also develop where some people seek gratification where they have no social sexual contacts in their lives.

This development of sexual fetish can be seen in the grim tale of Jerry Brudos, who went on to kill at least four women in Oregon between 1968 and 1969. His childhood tells us a little bit about how his fetish for shoes and women's clothes developed.

This fascination with women's shoes and their feet, would ultimately lead him to kill, in order to gratify himself and feed his fetish, where the desires were not being filled elsewhere. Jerry's life was bizarre, and so were the murders he committed.

A damaged brain

Born as Jerome Henry Brudos, in South Dakota in 1939, he was subjected to violent physical and emotional abuse by his mother, who wanted to have a daughter as her second child. She was so adamant about this that she was angry Jerry had turned out to be a boy.

From the age of five, after his mother moved him and his brother to Oregon, he developed his shoe fetish, and was once found in a junkyard playing with stiletto shoes while touching himself. He also stole women's underwear from washing lines and would wear them whenever he could.

At the age of seven, he attacked his female teacher and attempted to steal her shoes. This put him on the radar of a psychiatrist who was only granted minimal access to him, due to his mother blocking any therapy.

Around the same time, he was known to dress in women's clothes and he developed a female personality that would help him cope with the reality of his life. By his early teens, he was in and out of therapy and was becoming frustrated.

His frustration turned to anger, and from the age of 15, he began to stalk girls and women. Soon after, he began attacking them. He attacked at least three women by pushing them to the ground, choking them to unconsciousness, then eloping – with their shoes.

Overpowering fetish

At the age of 17, in Oregon, he dragged a young women into a remote area and beat her before threatening her with a knife. He ordered her to strip and perform sexual acts on him before escaping once again with her shoes. She was able to identify him and he was arrested shortly after.

He was admitted to a psychiatric hospital for almost a year. There, he was diagnosed with schizophrenia, and psychiatrists learned that his sexual fantasies revolved around his hatred towards his mother and females in general.

When he was released, he managed to live a relatively normal life for a number of years. He became an electrician, and at age 21, married a 17-year-old girl named Darcie. Together they would have two children, but soon enough, the gratification was fading and Jerry's fetish returned – ten-fold.

He began ordering Darcie to do her chores and housework naked – except for a pair of high heels. She obeyed her husband, and he was free to take photographs of her legs and shoes as she cleaned and cooked for him in the nude.

It remains unclear whether Darcie knew of his overpowering fetish beforehand and if she agreed to it or was forced. Still, his fetish became clearer when he became a transvestite and insisted on wearing Darcie's clothes around the house, while she was forced to wear none.

Then in 1968, age 29, the abuse from all those years ago, combined with the intense sexual desire for women's shoes, led Jerry to commit murder.

Opportunistic killing

The first murder came from an unfortunate circumstance, an opportunistic killing that set in place a turn of events leading to multiple murders. On 26th January 1968, 19-year-old encyclopedia salesperson Linda Slawson, made the mistake of knocking on Jerry's door.

Despite his mother and his children being in the house at the time, Jerry lured Linda to the basement where he knocked her out with a plank of wood. While she was unconscious, he strangled her to death.

After many hours of posing her corpse in sexual positions, and dressing her up in his own women's clothes, he sawed off her left foot. He wrapped it up and kept it in the basement freezer, before disposing of Linda's body in the nearby Willamette River.

The taste for murder had taken hold but he wanted his next victim to be as easy to lure as Linda. 10 months later, to the day, on 26th November, he spotted a broken-down car and offered to give the woman, 23-year-old Jan Whitney, a lift to his home.

Before he got home, he pulled over, strangled her and raped her corpse. He took the body home with him and hung her from a pulley in the garage for the next four days. He dressed the corpse in women's clothes, engaged in necrophilia, and photographed her.

Shortly before disposing of her body in the Willamette River, he cut off one of her breasts and made a plastic mould with it. He filled the mould with resin and used it as a paperweight.

Out of control

The investigation into the women's disappearances had already begun but with no bodies as evidence, the police were at a loss, leaving Jerry to continue killing. Realising other victims may not be so easy to come by, he resorted to forced abductions.

On 27th March 1969, while dressed as a woman, he abducted 18-year-old Karen Sprinker from a shopping centre car park. As with Whitney, he strangled her to death then hung her from a pulley in his garage, before engaging in necrophilia, and dressing her in various women's clothing. He also cut of both her breasts and made plastic moulds of them, before dumping her body in the same river.

The longer he got away with murder, the shorter the time between victims, and the desire to gratify himself intensified. On the 21st and 22nd of April, he attempted to abduct a 24-year-old woman and then a 15-year-old girl, but he failed in his attempts.

On the third day, 23rd April, he abducted 22-year-old Linda Salee from another shopping mall car park. He killed her and hung her from the same pulley in his garage. This time, he experimented on her, in a bizarre attempt to reanimate her corpse.

He ran multiple electrical currents through Linda's body, in an effort to restart her heart and brain. When this failed, he tied her body to an engine-part of a car and dumped her body in the Willamette River. Meanwhile, the net was closing in on Jerry.

Caught with photos

Two weeks later, a fisherman on his usual route along the Willamette, discovered two bodies in the river. Police quickly learned they were the bodies of Sprinker and Salee but due to the decomposition, there was minimal evidence to work with.

As they appealed for witnesses at a nearby university campus, some students came forward and told them of a creepy guy. They described Jerry in detail and told police he would act strange around some of the female students, while lusting over their shoes, and would sometimes be dressed as a woman.

One female student claimed that Jerry would constantly push her to go on a date with him but she refused. At one point, he had got hold of her phone number and would ring non-stop. Police then decided to put a sting operation in place.

They asked the student to phone Jerry and agree to go on a date with him. When Jerry arrived at the meeting point, police met him and interrogated him about the murders. Initially he gave a fake address but they quickly found out where he really lived.

Upon entering his garage, they found various pieces of evidence, including a cutting tool that had the same serrated edges as the tool used to cut the cords that were wrapped around the bodies. Then they found items of clothing – and shoes belonging to the victims.

And if that wasn't enough, they opened a drawer that contained hundreds of photos of Jerry posing with the corpses of three of his victims. He was arrested on the spot and immediately confessed.

Shoe catalogues

In June 1969, Jerry was found guilty of three first-degree murders. He admitted to killing his first victim, Slawson, but because he had taken no photos with her, and her body was never recovered, prosecutors were not able to convict him.

However, there were photos of Slawson's left foot, but because there were no personal photographs of Slawson that showed her bare-footed, and with the foot dumped in the river too, there was no way to prove the foot belonged to Slawson.

The body of Whitney, his second victim, was found many months after Jerry's ultimate conviction of her murder. Darcie was arrested and questioned about any knowledge she had of the murders, but she told investigators that she was under the control of her husband and had to follow his orders.

With regards to the garage, Jerry had told her it was off-limits and she was not to enter without his permission. If she needed access, she had call him on the intercom. Unbeknownst to Darcie, the bodies of his victims might have been hanging in the garage, while she was doing her chores in the nude.

A witness came forward to claim she had seen both Jerry and Darcie carrying what looked like a mannequin into the garage one day, and later thought it could have been a body. But the evidence wasn't strong enough and Darcie was released. It is possible that she assisted her husband while under his control but it has never been proven.

Despite many appeals, and claims of having no memory of the attacks, Jerry was sentenced to life in prison, where he died of liver cancer in 2006, aged 67.

When his cell was cleaned out, guards found piles of women's shoe catalogues – that Jerry had been collecting to gratify his eternal fetish.

Killings of Templeton Woods

After the first Templeton Woods murder, girls stopped walking the streets alone, after the second, the area became ground zero for Britain's most infamous cold case, with links to the Zodiac Killer.

Templeton Woods

Located a short drive north of Dundee City Centre, in Scotland, Templeton Woods is considered a great place to visit for walking, cycling, horse riding, picnics, or to watch the wonderful wildlife that lives there. You might even spot a red squirrel or two!

Templeton Woods is a relatively small council wood, covering an area of just under 150 acres, dwarfed by some of Scotland's larger landscapes. Surprising then that the woods are known across the world, not as a place of beauty, but of murder.

From 1979 to 1987, three murders of young women took place in and near the woods, and although one of them appeared to be solved, the other two remain a mystery to this day.

Combined with reports of women being attacked there as recently as 2017, then perhaps it's no surprise why Templeton Woods is draped in such infamy and terror.

1979

As a schoolgirl, Carol Lannen didn't leave much of an impression on her peers at the time, she was a quiet girl who kept herself to herself and didn't have many friends to shout about. However, her death at the age of 18, did leave an impression.

On 21st March 1979, prostitute Carol got into a red estate car on Exchange Street in Dundee City and it was the last time anyone saw her alive – apart from her killer. The next day, her nude body was found near a picnic table in Templeton Woods. She had been tied up and strangled to death.

As the police investigation grew, other prostitutes were able to describe the driver of the red car to police. Over 6,000 owners of red cars were interviewed and an artist-sketch of the suspect, based on the witness accounts, was released to the public.

11 days later, her personal belongings and clothes were found on the side of River Don, over 70 miles away, north of Aberdeen. The murder of Carol Lannen changed the way teenage girls in Dundee conducted themselves, according to recent interviews of women who were teenagers at the time.

And like many crimes in the 1970s, the case went cold and the murder went unsolved, a dark footnote to cap off a year of change for the country. Until 1980, when a second murder in Templeton Woods rocked Dundee and the whole of Scotland.

1980

As a trainee nursery nurse, 20-year-old Elizabeth McCabe needed to let her hair down occasionally. In February 1980, she and a friend went out drinking in popular bars around Dundee. She left a nightclub in the early hours of 11th February – and never made it home.

She was reported missing by her family the same morning. Two weeks later, on the day of what would have been her 21st Birthday, Elizabeth's body was found by two rabbit hunters out walking their dogs, who initially thought they had unearthed a mannequin.

When police arrived, they found her partially nude body in the undergrowth. She had been strangled to death, just 150 metres away from where Carol's body was discovered 11 months earlier. When the newspapers got hold of it and linked it to the 1979 death, the *Templeton Woods Murders* were birthed into existence.

With the severe possibility that a serial attacker was loose in Dundee, the police launched what would become the largest murder investigation the region had ever seen. An estimated 7,500 people were interviewed, and the records of every accommodation owner in the city were scoured for clues.

But as in the death of Carol Lannen, the case went cold – until 2005. Using new forensic techniques, former taxi driver Vincent Simpson was arrested and charged with Elizabeth's murder, based on the evidence that his DNA was found on a blue jumper near the body – which may or may not have had anything to do with the murder.

Unsurprisingly, after a seven-week trial, the jury found Simpson not guilty. The police admitted the evidence had been fundamentally flawed and potentially contaminated. However, the police were known to have fixated their efforts on taxi drivers in the city to such an extent that they took manpower away from other possibilities.

And so it was that Elizabeth McCabe's murder fell into the realm of the unsolved the same way Carol's had.

But in 1987, a murder in nearby Melville Lower Wood, led to an altogether different suspect.

1987

30-year-old Lynda Hunter worked with the Samaritans and was a qualified social worker who disappeared on 21st August 1987. The next day, her husband, Andrew Hunter, officially reported her missing.

Immediately, due to his suspicious nature, Andrew became the suspect in her disappearance but the police needed more evidence – or a body – to charge him with anything. They began investigating his life and pulling the pieces apart.

Andrew was a voluntary worker at the Salvation Army, where he had met Lynda via the Samaritans, and they had an affair while he was still married. In December 1984, his wife, Christine, died of suicide, found hanging by a noose in the attic of her home.

During his relationship with Lynda, he took a gay lover and visited gay saunas in Glasgow and Edinburgh. He was also known to every prostitute in Dundee, becoming a regular client to many, and to top it off, he had a 22-year-old drug addicted girlfriend on the side.

Seven months after her disappearance, Lynda's body was found in Melville Lower Wood, in Ladybank, Fife, just 18 miles from Templeton Woods. She had been strangled with her dog lead. Police swooped in on Andrew Hunter and arrested him for her murder.

Despite pleading his innocence, Andrew was charged and ultimately convicted of Lynda's murder in 1988.

Andrew had killed her because she became pregnant and he dumped her body in the woods to hide the evidence. Just five years later, in 1993, Andrew died of a heart attack while in prison.

But some suggest he had taken many secrets to the grave.

Enter the sleuths

Hunter's case had gained considerable interest across the entire United Kingdom, as it was the first Scottish case to be shown on the national Crimewatch program in 1987. Because of that, Andrew was linked to the Templeton Woods murders, not least because of his regular visits to Dundee.

The description of the driver given to police by witnesses in the Carol Lannen case seemed to be a strikingly close fit to that of Hunter. He was also known to have abused his wife, and Lynda, along with having a penchant for walks through local woods and fetishized sex.

While many have linked him with the Templeton Woods murders, he never gave any inclination he was involved, and any supposed evidence against him has washed away with time.

Interestingly, the authorities have closed the cases and have no new plans to reopen them but it hasn't stopped an army of online sleuths and researchers attempting to solve them. So, who was responsible for the Templeton Woods murders?

World's End murders

In October 1977, 18 months before Carol Lannen's death, two 17-year-old girls were murdered on different nights in Edinburgh, 60 miles from Dundee. They were both last seen leaving the World's End Pub in the city's old town. Their killer was Angus Sinclair.

He had previously killed his eight-year-old neighbour in 1961, for which he served 10 years inside. In 1982, he pleaded guilty to the rape and assault of 11 children aged six to 14 and was sentenced to life in prison.

In 2001, he was first charged with the World's End murders, but after various controversies with botched forensics, he was acquitted. An amendment to the double jeopardy law later saw him convicted of the murders in 2014, along with the 1978 murder of 17-year-old Mary Gallacher in Glasgow.

Then, he was linked to four other young women killed in Scotland between 1977 and 1978, leading to some suspecting he was the Templeton Woods murderer. But police records show that Sinclair was in custody for a firearms charge at the time of both women's deaths.

However, many prisoners were allowed out on work release, with much of the work release program going unrecorded in the late 1970s.

Partner in crime

Sinclair was so certain about the similarities between the murders that he feared being charged with both

Templeton Woods deaths, due to the circumstantial evidence. Carol's purse and clothing were found on the riverbank near Aberdeen, a city where Sinclair was working in a motel before his firearm arrest – and after.

The photofit was a close match to his appearance, and the fact he had been convicted of four murders and multiple rapes, led some to believe he was the killer. But if Sinclair was in custody at the time, and had not been given work release – which is unrecorded – then who killed them?

Sinclair was known to have a partner in crime, named Gordon Hamilton, who helped him lure his victims, and also killed on his own. Could it be that the Templeton Woods deaths were copycat killings, designed to look like the World's End murders, to cover Sinclair's tracks?

Whatever further secrets Sinclair had, died with him in 2019, while serving his sentence.

Zodiac Killer

For many, the Zodiac Killer is one of the most infamous cold cases in America, if not the world. Between December 1968 and October 1969, in San Francisco, five people were killed by an unidentified serial killer.

The killer gave himself the moniker of Zodiac by sending taunting letters to local newspapers, many of which contained strange ciphers and codes. In one of the letters, the killer claimed to have murdered 37 victims.

After the last known murder, the Zodiac Killer disappeared and theories about what happened to him have perpetuated online. Other murders across the world have been connected to the Zodiac Killer, including sprees in Italy, Germany, and for some – Scotland.

In 2009, Tayside Major Crimes Investigations received a dossier that had been researched by an unidentified author, claiming that the Zodiac Killer had left California for Scotland in the mid-1970s, and that he was still living in the country.

Zodiac's last act

The conveniently unknown author claimed to have identified an American man living in the north-east of Scotland as the prime suspect in the Zodiac killings. According to the author's research, the man was responsible for Carol's death, and suspected in Elizabeth's.

In 2015, the author sent an email to a Scottish newspaper, and with regards to Carol's murder, claimed, *'this criminal act is often referred to as the first of 'The Templeton Woods Murders' my research formed a case study, which I submitted to Tayside CID in October 2009.'*

'As a result, an investigation was carried out into the suspect. Although stood down after six months, the suspect remains, to this day, 'under review'. There was no sex on the agenda, and it appears that empowerment was the motive. This I believe, was Zodiac's last act and had a different motive to the crimes in California.'

Though the Templeton Woods murder cases are seen as closed, authorities continue to log any new information that comes in. The killings could have been carried out by the Zodiac Killer, Angus Sinclair's partner, or an unidentified local man.

Perhaps the murders of Carol and Elizabeth were unconnected and it was merely a coincidence they were found so close together. Their deaths remain unsolved, and their killer or killers unidentified. Though it doesn't stop bizarre theories continuing to be talked about.

Templeton Woods continues to haunt investigators and true crime fans, as it has done for the past 40 years. It is one of Scotland's most infamous cold cases, and as time ticks on, the window for solving it gets ever smaller.

The Real 'Orphan'

Straight out of the Hollywood horror 'Orphan', a loving couple adopt a young girl, only to discover she is an adult, who stands at the end of their bed at night, holding a knife.

Mission of love

What began as a mission of love when a couple adopted a small child from the Ukraine, turned into something out of a horror movie, when the child began threatening to kill them, and stood at the end of their bed with a knife.

As time went on, the adoptive parents discovered that the child they had adopted was an adult posing as a child. In fear of their lives, they set her up with her own home and ran as far away from her as they could.

Five years later, the couple were arrested on charges of child neglect, but they had a court letter confirming that their eight-year-old adopted daughter was in fact a 22-year-old adult at the time they were looking after her.

Suddenly, the world's media and medical professionals were lining up to see what the hell was going on. No-one could agree whether the girl was a child or an adult, despite medical tests. The girl claimed she was neglected by a family she loved. The couple claimed she was evil personified.

You're going to want to strap in for this one.

Adoption

Kristine and Michael Barnett were experienced foster parents who ran a children's day care centre in Westfield, Indiana. Kristine had also written a book on how to cope with children with ADHD, following her own experiences.

In May 2010, the couple agreed to the emergency adoption of a Ukrainian-born six-year-old girl named Natalia Grace, who they collected from Florida. Her adoption was completed six months later and the Barnett's became her official guardians.

As with all their foster children, the Barnett's treated Natalia as if she were their own daughter, as Kristine couldn't have children of her own. Natalia had a bone growth disorder which causes a form of dwarfism, resulting in a short stature, skeletal abnormalities, and problems with vision.

But from the offset, things seemed a little strange compared to the other children they had adopted. They had only 24 hours to complete the paperwork for the emergency adoption, and as such, Natalia's details were few and far between.

It appeared she had been in the United States since 2008 and had a Ukrainian birth certificate that stated she was born in September 2003. It materialised that she needed a home immediately because her previous foster family had given her up – for reasons which have never been disclosed.

Threats and fear

The Barnett's were already beginning to question how old Natalia really was. When Kristine bathed Natalia for the first time, she was met with a full bloom of pubic hair, and signs that the girl had recently been menstruating.

She also had adult teeth, and never grew an inch taller, which even for those suffering from dwarfism was considered weird. One day at the beach, despite struggling to walk, Natalia had stood up straight and ran into the water.

Four months later, when she turned seven-years-old, Natalia began opening up and becoming more confident around her new family. When she spoke, her vocabulary and language skills were far beyond that of a young child, but she had no trace of a Ukrainian accent – nor could she speak the language.

Then things became dangerous for the Barnett's. Natalia was enrolled at school in December 2010, and on the way there, Kristine claimed that Natalia deliberately tried to push her into an electric fence. And that was the beginning of Natalia's so-called campaign of terror towards the family.

On one occasion, she sprayed bleach into Kristine's coffee, along with the words '*I am trying to poison you.*' She was known to talk about killing them and their other adoptive children, with details like rolling them up in a blanket and burying them in the backyard.

Many sleepless nights were had when the Barnett's awoke in the darkness to find Natalia standing at the edge of their bed with a knife in her hand. They had to hide all the sharp objects in the house, but Natalia was known to have hidden a knife above the fridge as a back-up.

Natalia was also prone to jumping out of moving cars and smearing her own blood on mirrors around the home. She also kept the company of teenage girls and refused to play with children's toys. One time, Kristine was watching a baby monitor camera, and gasped in horror when Natalia slapped a baby boy, as she thought no-one was watching.

An adult in their midst

In 2011, in fear of their lives, they took Natalia to a mental health specialist, to work out what was going on. The specialist confirmed that Natalia had a severe psychological illness only diagnosed in adults, and determined that Natalia was in fact, an adult.

Natalia then spent many weeks at the St Vincent Indianapolis Stress Center, a state-run institute for psychiatric disorders. There, it was said that Natalia confessed to being far older than she appeared, at least 18 according to one psychiatrist report.

In March 2012, a physician involved with the Barnett's and Natalia, confirmed that the 2003 birth certificate was vastly inaccurate, and that Natalia may have made a career out of pretending to be a child, fooling the entire system.

In June 2012, with the backing of the mental health team, the Barnett's mounted a court case to have Natalia's birth certificate changed to reflect her true age. Bone density tests established that Natalia was at least 16.

Marion County Superior Court in Indianapolis, Indiana, delivered a legal ruling that Natalia was actually born in 1989, based on medical evidence. Astonishingly, this put her age at 22 when she had been adopted by the Barnett's.

Now having evidence that Natalia was not a child, the Barnett's made plans to be rid of her, but they kept to their moral code of looking after those less fortunate. In 2013, when Natalia was 9 – or 23 – they set her up with her own apartment and life, then moved to Canada one month later.

Natalia was looked after by a community mental health and social team who helped her get a social security number and checked in on her to see how she was coping living alone.

There, it appears the story might have ended, but five years later, police tracked down the Barnett's – and arrested them on suspicion of child neglect and abandonment.

Orphan

For five years, Natalia had lived in the apartment by herself, cooking, cleaning, and getting on with her life, when one day she told police she had been abandoned by her adoptive parents. The Barnett's were arrested and charged with neglect.

But despite the accusations of child abuse, the Barnett's had something up their sleeve that would confuse everyone and lead them down the same rabbit hole we've just been on. How can it be child abuse – when there is no child?

Kristine and Michael, who divorced shortly after moving to Canada, fought back against the accusations and stated that they in fact were the victims. They countered Natalia's case and claimed they were victims of fraud because the girl was an adult con artist who was trying to kill them.

In 2009, ten years before the Barnett's case was made public, the film 'Orphan' was released. The film's plot is remarkably similar. *'After losing their baby, a couple adopt a nine-year-old girl. However, they soon make a troubling discovery about her mysterious past and uncover several traits of her disturbing personality.'*

The girl in the film, Esther, played by Isabelle Fuhrman, is discovered to be a 33-year-old Russian woman posing as a child to work her way into loving families. She had killed her previous foster family and tries to murder her new one. Despite itself being based on a true story, the details of the Natalia case were strikingly similar.

Back and forth

Kristine claimed that they had not abandoned Natalia and had kept in contact to see how she was doing as an adult. They paid for the lease on the apartment to stop her being homeless and did everything possible to make sure she was safe.

When Natalia stopped making contact, Kristine worried she had been adopted by another family, but still lived in fear of waking up in the middle of the night and seeing Natalia standing at the end of her bed with a knife. In 2019, Kristine and Michael went to trial individually.

Natalia, with her new adoptive family, went on the Dr. Phil show in America to explain that she was only a child. However, the Dr. Phil appearance backfired, with many experts claiming she was displaying adult behaviour, and not that of the 16-year-old she reported to be.

The cases against the Barnett's were ultimately thrown out due to the statute of limitations being passed. Their lawyers also argued that Natalia was legally considered an adult by the state of Indiana, was legally responsible for herself, and had the legal papers to prove it.

The orphan case remains bizarre

The Barnett's were described as exemplary foster parents, having raised child genius Jake Barnett, who had his first academic paper published at the age of 12. It was clear they had an impressive passion and aptitude for raising children who were not their own.

It would be a remarkable turn of events if the Barnett's had lied about Natalia's actions and age purely to be rid of any responsibility to her. Yet, it would be even more remarkable if a 22-year-old woman had posed as a child to infiltrate a loving family.

Medical results are frustrating, as where one bone density test showed she was an adult, another test brought up in the trial showed she was a child. Another report stated that when she was 16 on the Dr. Phil show, she was in fact 33.

The orphan case remains bizarre because the motives on both sides are not immediately obvious. Natalia found new adoptive parents, who rebuked any of the claims made by the Barnett's, including that she had periods. But maybe Natalia was clever enough to hide them from her new family.

Despite many appeals by her adoptive parents, Natalia's date of birth has never been changed back. The original Marion County Superior Court verdict in 2012, showing that Natalia was in fact born in 1989, and not 2003, remains the official legal verdict of her age.

The undisclosed reasons why her first foster family gave her up, remain a mystery to this day – if of course, they were her first foster family.

Case of the Lego Kleptomaniac

A fraudster used an unusual method to illegally purchase Lego sets, to sell on eBay, but he didn't need the money, as he was a multi-millionaire vice president of a Silicon Valley software giant.

SAP

In 2012, an unusual criminal was targeting toy shops in California, mostly the Target stores; a large general merchandise retailer. The crimes went unrecorded for many weeks until shop workers and the loss-prevention teams became suspicious of his purchases.

When managers of the stores latched onto one individual, they informed security to watch him to see if they could confirm their suspicions. Soon after, he was caught and taken away in a police car.

But when he was arrested, it turned out the man didn't exactly need the money, as he was the vice-president of SAP; a global software company based in Silicon Valley.

'SAP is one of the world's leading producers of software for the management of business processes, developing solutions that facilitate effective data processing and information flow across organisations.' It's all a rather technical way of saying; they make barcodes and test software.

Yet, SAP is one of the leading software companies in the world and served 47-year-old Thomas Langenbach well. He had a sprawling mansion, strong family and social connections, and a solid career. What exactly did he do that got him caught and why did he do it?

Fraud in motion

Thomas was a life-long fan of Lego, proclaiming it to be his one true passion, and he would buy new sets as often as he could. He also sold some of his older sets on eBay. But then a lightbulb went off in his head and he decided to combine the research of SAP with his Lego hobby.

Realising that sales in stores were basically run through a data system, he worked out Target's barcode structure and began printing off fake barcodes. He tested it out the first time on an inexpensive Lego set, covering up the real barcode with one of his perfectly designed fake ones.

When he took it to the checkout, the cashier simply scanned it through and Thomas paid a small percentage of the real cost. Though he wasn't strapped for cash, he then sold the set on eBay for a profit.

Seeing that the scam worked and having found a way to purchase and keep the more popular Lego sets, and sell on the rest, he did it again, and again. Until the employees at the various Target stores began noticing a pattern.

It wasn't unusual for someone to buy lots of Lego, the brand of building blocks remains one of the most popular toys in the world with children and collectors. It was unusual that the pricing was way off from what other people were paying.

Tom's Brick Yard

When Target saw a pattern of expensive Lego sets being purchased much lower than the retail price, at levels that would lose them money, they looked closer at the CCTV footage. But although Thomas was acting suspicious on each occasion, there wasn't anything obvious going on.

At one store that he regularly visited, the manager asked the security guard to find out what he was doing. On 8th May 2012, the guard watched Thomas covertly cover the original barcode with one of his fake ones, while he was holding the box of Lego close to the display.

Thomas had been caught red-handed but the security waited until he paid for it. Upon walking out the store, he was apprehended, and the police were called. Inside his car, they found a bag with thousands of different barcodes.

It turned out that the vice-president of SAP had been using his skills to full effect. The barcodes were so well-designed that on the checkout screen, it still showed the item he was purchasing in real life.

He bought a $279 box of Millennium Falcon Lego for only $49 but at the checkout it still showed up as Millennium Falcon Lego. When police raided his sprawling mansion, they found stacks of Lego and other toys that he had listed and sold on eBay, with one officer saying it looked like a mini-Legoland.

It was estimated Thomas had made $30,000 from the scam by selling the expensive ones on eBay. Due to the number of barcodes they found in the car, it was suspected he was attempting to fraudulently purchase thousands of Lego boxes. His eBay name was 'tomsbrickyard'.

Bricking it

But why? That was the question on everyone's lips. Why did a multi-millionaire decide to run a scam on Lego sets that would only net him tens of dollars at a time? Thomas had been with SAP since the early days of 1988, and moved to the Silicon Valley lab in 2000, twelve years before his arrest.

The guy was considered a genius, he had a computer science degree and was one of the top dogs in a vast software empire. Though initially pleading not guilty at his trial, it was suggested he make a plea deal to avoid five years in prison.

He accepted a plea deal and was found guilty of fraud and theft, sentenced to one month in jail, another five months under house arrest, and three years' probation. Unsurprisingly, he was sacked from his position at SAP while he was in prison, which cost him his house and livelihood.

Thomas was reported as saying that he switched the barcodes out of curiosity, to see if it really worked. He also wanted to see if the customer price scanner and cash-register scanner priced the items the same or cheaper. At the same time, he denied swapping the barcodes on other items.

Clearly he did, and if the first sale gratified his curiosity – and he got away with it, then he would have continued, believing himself to be untouchable. Due to being in his job for so long, he may also have acted out of boredom, but mostly it was seen as compulsion.

The motive in this instance wasn't money but as a result of kleptomania, which is classified in psychiatry as an impulse control disorder, part of the OCD spectrum. It is defined as the inability to resist the urge to steal items, for reasons other than personal financial gain.

His eBay account pointed towards this, when it was revealed he didn't sell the Lego sets as new. Instead, he had opened them, built the set, and photographed it outside the box, before bagging it back up to sell on.

For Thomas Langenbach, his kleptomania meant he would never be able to 'Lego' of the past, forever bonded to the small bricks, that as it turned out were not such a good fit after all, and he alone was left to pick up the pieces.

Bumbling Burglar Trapped in Escape Room

A burglar broke into an escape room to rob the place, but when he went to leave, realised he quite literally couldn't escape, so had to call the police to come and rescue him.

Northwest Escape Experience

The Clark County Sheriff's department in Vancouver are used to bizarre phone calls and cases, but in 2018 when they got a phone call from a man claiming to be trapped, they were led down a rabbit hole of criminal errors and escape room culture.

On a warm Summers night at approximately 3am, the department received a call from a worried 40-year-old Rye Daniel Wardlaw, who had apparently fled a burglary and hid in his panic room – or so he said. When they traced the call, they learned he was phoning from inside the Northwest Escape Experience.

It's an escape room in a strip mall in the small town of Hazel Dell. The Northwest Escape Experience is popular with escape room tourists and players who want to challenge themselves to a series of riddles or puzzles in order to escape the room, or succession of rooms.

Unfortunately, for Wardlaw, the game was up before it even began.

Unusual story

Wardlaw had attempted to break in through the back door of the business but it was too strong to get through. He managed to get inside the retail and office park's electrical room and open a lockbox. There, he found a key to a suite that was located next door to the escape room but he needed to get into the building.

He punched a hole through the thin wall at the back of the electrical room and found his way to the bathroom of a physical therapy office – then he sat down to have a burrito that was waiting in his pocket.

He found a shared door between the two businesses and entered the escape room, knocking over storage lockers on his way in, which blocked the door from the other side.

As he walked around the escape room, he became disorientated and suddenly became frightened that he would be trapped in the room. He tried to leave by the door he had entered from but it wouldn't budge.

With no way out, Wardlaw dialled 911 and requested police assistance with an unusual story. He told them he was sleeping in his own home when burglars entered his property and so he fled to his place of business; the Northwest Escape Experience.

Due to the fact he had left in such a hurry, and the fear he felt because of the robbers in his house, he was stuck in his own business and couldn't get out, referring to the escape room as his own personal panic room.

Police asked him for his home address but the address didn't exist and the Sheriff's department dispatched officers to the escape room to find out what was going on.

Caught

Between the time the officers were dispatched and when they arrived, Wardlaw was so fearful that he had phoned the sheriff's department another three times out of fear of being trapped in the escape room forever.

When deputies arrived at the strip mall, they discovered the front door of the escape room experience was unlocked, and no one was inside. The call had been made using the reception phone inside the escape room. They then heard a crashing noise from behind the building itself and went to investigate.

One of the deputies jumped in his car and drove around to the other side of the building where he saw Wardlaw quickly walking away. When the deputy called out, Wardlaw dropped a mobile phone he had stolen from the escape room office.

The deputy ordered him to stop but Wardlaw claimed the phone was his and that he had not been anywhere near the building or the escape room, despite being right next door to the building. Wardlaw was arrested on the spot.

No escape

When the owners of the escape room, Tamara and Rob Bertrand, were told of the robbery a couple of hours later, they rushed to their business to see what had happened. Fortunately the damage was minimal and they were able to open the following day.

However, police needed to know why Wardlaw couldn't get out of the escape room. It turned out that all he had to do was turn the inside lock on the front door but he didn't know how to use the lock and thought he was trapped.

Shortly before police arrived, he had finally figured it out, but not before calling 911 four times in fear of his life.

Wardlaw was charged with three counts of second-degree burglary but at his trial claimed he was homeless and had nowhere else to go, despite stealing the phone and denying he had ever been in the escape room – probably to avoid more embarrassment of what had happened.

He then claimed he broke the handle on the building's back door and called 911 to report himself but got confused and made up a story. He also claimed he was checking to see if the gas was working as part of a safety check.

Beyond spinning tales of untruths, Wardlaw was convicted of robbery and handed down a fine. Despite being angry with the damage to their small business, Tamara joked they now have a zero percent escape rate with criminals.

Bonus material

Movies that Influenced Killers

The influence of movies inspiring crime is still debated and argued over to this day. Most people who watch violent movies do not go on to re-enact what they might have seen. But there are some people that do. Before we look at some examples, let's take a closer look at the truth of it.

'Pornography and violence poison our music and movies and TV and video games. The Virginia Tech shooter, like the Columbine shooters before him, had drunk from this cesspool.' – Mitt Romney, during his presidential campaign.

Romney sat on the extreme side of the fence and was in effect blaming entertainment for the reasons behind violent crime.

Is the death of Simba's father in *The Lion King* any more violent than John McCLane taking out bad guys in *Die Hard*?

Apparently it's only one's opinion on things that makes a difference. The assertions that violent movies cause people to become violent has been around for quite some time and a lot of research has been written on the subject. The fear has always been that watching a violent movie will make someone violent in real life. The same has always been said about gaming.

However, in an article in the *Washington Post* by *Fareed Zakaria*, he claims that people should look to Japan as a counter-argument for any claims of entertainment influencing violence.

The Japanese are the biggest gaming-country in the world, when player and population ratio is looked at, yet the murder rate in Japan is close to zero. He put forward the argument that the main difference is the restrictions on firearms in Japan.

Many people want violent movies to be banned or at least restricted to a certain age group, which mostly they are. But some have claimed that it would mean censorship should reach all areas of entertainment, right down to fairy tales, which arguably have more written violence in them than most films.

On the flip-side, it has been proven that violent movies and games have more benefits than they do negatives. Researchers found that watching any type of movie, violent or not, can help people cope with their emotions. It can help people overcome challenging situations, expand their imagination, and relieve stress.

There is of course a bigger argument *against* the influence of movies on normal people. The people who go on to kill or commit crime after seeing a film were more likely to have been aggressive in the first instance.

Those who commit violent crime, including murder, already exhibited aggressive traits. Such attributes were predictive of criminal behaviour, and not the viewing of movies themselves. Movies might validate one's own beliefs, rather than changing them.

The Collector (1965)

This 1965 British film is said to have directly influenced a number of cases. Serial killer *Robert Andrew Berdella Jr.* AKA: *The Kansas City Butcher* remains one of the evilest killers in the modern era. His case was one of the first known instances of a movie directly impacting the thought processes of someone who had the potential to kill *and* would go on to kill.

The plot of *The Collector* is about a man who abducts women and holds them captive in his basement to add to his *collection*. It is a direct correlation to the exact process used by Berdella in his future murders. Except that he chose men instead of women. Berdella directly cited the film as an influence of how he could kill.

The Collector was also said to have influenced the serial killing duo *Leonard Lake* and *Charles Ng.* who together in the mid-1980s killed at least 11 people but was suspected to be 25. The pair built a bunker to imprison two of their female victims. They were planning on using them as sex slaves and housemaids. They documented some of their interactions on tapes but decided to murder them instead.

They had a self-built torture-chamber in a secluded area of forest which was home to a number of elaborate torture machines on the walls and all around. They had even built a dentist's chair used for restraining their victims.

Basketball Diaries (1995)

The film featured *Leonardo DiCaprio* as a basketball player who succumbs to heroin addiction. In a dream sequence he walks into his school wearing a black trench coat and carrying a shotgun. Then he massacres his classmates.

The 1996 school shooting carried out by *Barry Loukaitis*, was a virtual mirror to the scene in the film. He killed three people and injured more while walking through his school wearing a black trench coat. He was heard quoting lines from the film. In school shootings over the years that followed, many more would wear black trench coats.

It is suggested that these people would have done what they did anyhow, but they used certain entertainment mediums to provide the final inspiration.

Scream (1996)

In Belgium in 2001, *Thierry Jaradin*, a 24-year-old lorry driver lured and killed his 15-year-old neighbour, *Alisson Cambier*. She had visited Jaradin's house to swap some videotapes and have a chat. She then rejected his sexual advances and he excused himself shortly after.

He returned wearing a black robe and the 'ghostface' mask from the movie. He had two large kitchen knives in his hands as he lunged at Cambier. He stabbed her 30 times, and in doing so had ripped open the entire left side of her body. He then carried the mutilated corpse to his bed, slipped a rose into one of her hands, then called his father to confess.

In the 2006 murder of 16-year-old *Cassie Jo Stoddart*, Scream was cited yet again as a direct inspiration of the killing. After her boyfriend had left her home, two of her high school classmates went to her house and cut the power to the property. They then broke in and stabbed her at least 30 times. They had both planned the murder ahead of time and cited *Scream* and the *Columbine Massacre* as direct inspirations.

The Matrix (1999)

Unbelievably, the '*Matrix defence*' has become a real thing. The premise of the film is that our reality is not real, instead we live in a giant computer program that we only perceive to be real. Several killers used the logic that people who were killed were not real people.

In Sweden, exchange student *Vadim Mieseges* killed and dismembered his landlady. Upon his arrest he told police that he had been sucked into the Matrix. In 2002, murderer *Tonda Lynn Ansley* of Ohio, also killed her landlady by shooting her in the head. She was found not guilty by reason of insanity as she had used the Matrix defence.

Robocop 2 (1990)

American serial killer *Nathaniel White* from New York killed six females from 1991 to 1992. He beat and stabbed them to death while on parole. White already had an aggressive personality but claimed it was *Robocop 2* that inspired him to kill his first victim.

In the film, a victim's throat was cut and the knife slit down the chest to the stomach. White copied the exact same style of murder and then left the body in the same position as it had been left in the scene of the film. He was sentenced to 150 years in prison.

Interview with the Vampire (1994)

A day after *Daniel Sterling* had watched *Interview with the Vampire* at the cinema, he took on Vampiric tendencies. *Lisa Stellwagen* had seen the film with him and visited him again the next day at his home.

He told her that he was going to kill her and savour her blood. Then he stabbed her seven times and drank her blood for several minutes. Stellwagen survived and her testimony sent Sterling to prison. Sterling later claimed that he enjoyed the movie but wouldn't blame his attack on it.

Bitesize Extras

Pizza Stalker

In the town of Dortmund, Germany, in 2018, lawyer Guido Grolle received a pizza delivered to his office by mistake. Which was fine, address errors were common. However, by the time he received over 100 pizzas, he realised he was being targeted.

Known as the first case of pizza stalking, a mystery person would deliberately order pizzas to be sent to Grolle's desk. He said, *'it's so irritating, I don't even get my work done anymore.'* Unfortunately, Grolle was having to pay for every delivery that showed up.

Sometimes while taking his morning shower, he'd get a notification on his phone from the office telling him a pizza was waiting for him. He'd scream into the shower curtain, knowing his day was about to ruined by multiple deliveries.

Police reported that Grolle wanted to press charges but didn't know who the person was. As the deliveries came from different takeaways around the city, the police struggled to find a suspect.

But for Grolle, it got worse when the pizza stalker changed his method and began delivering sushi, sausage and chips, and Greek food, to his office. Once Dortmund's takeaway's were informed of Grolle's address, they double-checked every order before it was made – only then did the orders stop coming in.

It remains unclear if the culprit was an unhappy client of Grolle's, or if he had ulterior motives. The pizza stalker remains unidentified.

Bank Robber Note Error

In 2019, in Cleveland, Ohio, 54-year-old Michael Harrell walked into a branch of the U.S. Bank and handed the bank teller a note. It stated that he was robbing the bank and informed the teller to hand over all the money.

The female bank teller looked at the note and realised it had been written on a document from the Ohio Bureau of Motor Vehicles – with Michael's name on it. She addressed Michael as Mr. Harrell then handed over some money from her cash drawer.

She called the police and gave them the note with Michael's name and address on it, and unsurprisingly, he was arrested the same afternoon. When they reviewed CCTV footage, it was shown that Michael didn't even cover his face and made no effort to conceal his identity.

An FBI agent said, '*when you present a note that has your name already on it, and address, it helps law enforcement tremendously.*'

Chicken Baron

To help win votes for his political seat in Romania, politician Florin Popescu, attempted to bribe his constituency with over 60 tonnes of fried chicken in 2012.

He distributed the chicken to the public in vans with the help of volunteers, in an area where he was attempting to become leader of the local council. After spending the equivalent of £85,000 ($120,000 USD) on fried chicken, he was arrested on suspicion of bribery.

Because he had distributed the chicken as a benefit of voting for him, it was seen also seen as electoral fraud. His case was taken to court where he was refused bail and charged with electoral fraud, breaking anti-corruption laws, and bribery.

He was sentenced to two years in prison and forced to resign from the political world. Despite numerous appeals, he served the whole of his sentence, and is now known as the Chicken Baron across Romania.

Bizarre True Crime Volume 1

Catch up today!

Bibliography

A selected bibliography and resource.

Ashford, B. (2019) *Mom says adopted Ukranian daughter, 9, was really deadly 22-year-old.* The Daily Mail. https://www.dailymail.co.uk/news/article-7479061/Mom-claims-Ukrainian-daughter-9-adopted-really-22-year-old-dwarfism.html

Associated Press. (2011) *Greece puts €1m bounty on bank robber accused of terrorism.* The Guardian. https://www.theguardian.com/world/2011/feb/09/greece-one-million-euro-reward

BBC News. (2020) *Jessie Earl murder: Fresh inquest bid over 1980s death.* https://www.bbc.co.uk/news/uk-england-53152687

Bell, Jennifer. (2012) *DNA breakthrough in Sutton Bank body case.* https://www.gazetteherald.co.uk/news/9588893.dna-breakthrough-in-1981-nude-in-the-nettles-case

Borland, B. (2015) *Zodiac Killer linked to Scots murder mystery.* https://www.express.co.uk/scotland/552679/Killer-Linked-Scots-murder

Britannica. *Affair of the Poisons.* French history. https://www.britannica.com/event/Affair-of-the-Poisons

Brooke, C. (2012) *'Nude in the nettles' body to be exhumed in bid to solve 30-year mystery of how she died.*

https://www.dailymail.co.uk/news/article-2084287/Nude-nettles-body-woman-exhumed-bid-solve-30-year-mystery-died.html

Cassata, Cathy. (2019) *Sexual Fetishes: What Causes Them?* Healthline. https://www.healthline.com/health-news/what-causes-sexual-fetishes

CBS News (2007) *Medicine Hat girl guilty of first-degree murder.* https://web.archive.org/web/20130916075740/http://www.cbc.ca/news/canada/calgary/medicine-hat-girl-guilty-of-first-degree-murder-1.640437

Chalmers, Phil. (2009) *Inside the Mind of a Teen Killer.* Thomas Nelson Inc. ISBN: 9781595551528

City Data. (2021) *Crime in Baltimore, Maryland (MD): murders, rapes, robberies, assaults... crime map.* http://www.city-data.com/crime/crime-Baltimore-Maryland.html

Daily Mail, The. (2012) *Silicon Valley vice president 'made fake bar codes to steal THOUSANDS of boxes of Lego from Target... and then sell them on eBay for $30,000'.* https://www.dailymail.co.uk/news/article-2148074/Silicon-Valley-tech-executive-Thomas-Langenbach-caught-switching-bar-codes-steal-Lego-Target.html

Daily News Egypt. (2016) *The Battle of Larnaca: Egypt's raid on the Cypriot airport in 1978.* Daily News Egypt. https://dailynewsegypt.com/2016/03/29/battle-larnaca-egypts-raid-cypriot-airport-1978

Department of Justice, U.S. Attorney's Office. (2019) *Press release: District Man Sentenced to 17 Years in Prison for 2016 Murder in Southeast Washington.* https://www.justice.gov/usao-dc/pr/district-man-sentenced-17-years-prison-2016-murder-southeast-washington

Elkind, Peter (May 1990). *The Curse of the Black Lords.* Texas Monthly. Vol. 18 no. 5.

Goldenberg, Sara. (2020) *Uncovering lies to solve a cold case: Experts reveal challenges at CrowdSolve.* Cleveland 19 News. https://www.cleveland19.com/2020/02/28/uncovering-lies-solve-cold-case-experts-reveal-challenges-crowdsolve/

Grann, David. *A postmodern murder mystery.* (2008) The New Yorker, Feb 11 & 18, 2008.

Green, Cham. *The Bodies of Leakin Park - Baltimore.* Retrieved 20 September 2021. http://chamspage.blogspot.com/

Hamilton, Lindsey. (2019) *After Templeton Woods murder, girls stopped walking the streets alone says Dundee woman.* https://www.eveningtelegraph.co.uk/fp/after-templeton-woods-murder-girls-stopped-walking-the-streets-alone-says-dundee-woman

Herman, Eleanor. (2009) *Sex with Kings: 500 Years of Adultery, Power, Rivalry, and Revenge.* HarperCollins. ISBN 978-006175155-4.

Hong, Sungook. (2010) *Wireless: From Marconi's Black-Box to the Audion.* The MIT Press. ISBN: 9780262514194

Horsnell, Michael. (2000) *Death in 1980 now murder inquiry.* Times. Gale Academic OneFile. https://go.gale.com/ps/anonymous?id=GALE%7CIF0501333417

Iscan, Mehmet Yasar. Helmer, Richard. (1993) *Craniofacial Image Analysis and Reconstruction. Forensic Analysis of the Skull: Craniofacial Analysis, Reconstruction, and Identification.* New York. Wiley-Liss.

James, Bill. James, Rachel McCarthy. (2017) *The Man from the Train.* New York. Scribner. ISBN: 9781476796253

Kindall, James. (1978) *Sword heist still baffles police.* Kansas City Star (online), 24th Sep 1978. 152.

Labby, Brian. (2016) *J.R., who helped kill her Medicine Hat family at age 12, freed after 10-year sentence.* CBC News. https://www.cbc.ca/news/canada/calgary/jr-medicine-hat-murders-steinke-sentence-review-1.3568118

Larson, Erik. (2006) *Thunderstruck.* Crown Publishing Group. ISBN: 9781400080663

McCloskey, Jimmy. (2018) *Burglar breaks into escape room and has to call police when he gets stuck.*

https://metro.co.uk/2018/07/11/burglar-breaks-escape-room-call-police-gets-stuck-7704378/

Metro, The. (2007) *Man cleared of 1980 woods murder.* https://metro.co.uk/2007/12/13/man-cleared-of-1980-woods-murder-583906

Nast, C. (2013). *Former SAP Exec Gets Prison Time for Lego Price Switcharoo.* https://www.wired.com/2013/08/langenbach/

Papenfuss, Mary. (2016) *US: Man under house arrest commits murder after he removes fake leg with ankle monitor.* https://www.ibtimes.co.uk/us-man-under-house-arrest-commits-murder-after-he-removes-fake-leg-attached-ankle-monitor-1566968

Psychology Today. (2019) *Fetishistic Disorder.* https://www.psychologytoday.com/gb/conditions/fetishistic-disorder

Reid, Cat. McCormick, Lisa. (2021) *Former Harry S. Truman Library and Museum employee reflects on 1978 heist of swords, daggers.* https://www.kshb.com/news/local-news/investigations/former-harry-s-truman-library-and-museum-employee-reflects-on-1978-heist-of-swords-daggers

Remington, Robert. Zickefoose, Sherri. (2009) *Runaway Devil: How Forbidden Love Drove a 12-Year-Old to Murder Her Family.* McClelland & Stewart Ltd. ISBN: 9780771073601

Rodrigue, George. (1982) *The Rise and Fall of a North Dallas Cult.* D Magazine. Dec 1982.

Rule, Ann. (1994) *Lust Killer.* Penguin Publishers. ISBN: 9780451166876

SAP. (2021) *What is SAP? Company information.* https://www.sap.com/about/company/what-is-sap.html

Shulman, Terrence Daryl (2004). *Something for Nothing: Shoplifting Addiction & Recovery.* Haverford, PA: Infinity Publishing. ISBN 0741417790.

Sierra Wireless. (2021) *Omnilink, Offender Monitoring Solution.* https://www.sierrawireless.com/products-and-solutions/managed-iot-services/omnilink-offender-monitoring-solution/

Traynor, Ian. (2007) *Polish author jailed over killing he used as plot.*
https://www.theguardian.com/world/2007/sep/06/books.booksnews

Truman Library Institute. (2021) *Renovation Timeline - Truman Library Institute.*
https://www.trumanlibraryinstitute.org/renovation-timeline/page/2/

Trust, W. (2021). *Visiting Templeton Woods.*
https://www.woodlandtrust.org.uk/visiting-woods/woods/templeton-woods

Villisca Ax Murder House. *The official website for the Villisca Ax Murder House.* https://www.villiscaiowa.com

Wilkins, Ron. (2021). *Prosecutors appeal order to dismiss neglect charges against Michael and Kristine Barnett.* Lafayette Journal & Courier.
https://eu.jconline.com/story/news/crime/2020/09/04/michael-and-kristine-barnett-still-face-neglect-charges-during-appeal/5715151002/

Wilkinson, Dr Caroline. (2004) *Forensic Facial Reconstruction.* Cambridge University Press.

Wren, Christopher S. (1978) *Egyptian Says Commandos Struck After 'Unnecessary' Cypriot Delay.* The New York Times.
https://www.nytimes.com/1978/02/22/archives/new-jersey-pages-egyptian-says-commandos-struck-after-unnecessary.htmlv

Photo and image credits:

Daria Głodowska, Rihaij, Enrique Meseguer, Pete Linforth, Evgeni Tcherkasski, Gerd Altmann, Walkers SK, Ray Shrewsberry, Karen Nadine, Stefan Keller, Dani Villar, Slon Pics, Tumisu, & Twelvetrees Camden.

Look for more in the Bizarre True Crime Series from Ben Oakley & Twelvetrees Camden

OUT NOW!

Printed in Great Britain
by Amazon

70551297R00112